Praise for

BREAKING THROUGH BIAS

and Andrea S. Kramer
and Alton B. Harris

"According to spouses Kramer and Harris, 'Women don't need to be fixed,' but society does, and quickly. The authors proceed to identify a serious advancement problem for women, who make up 45 percent of entry-level professionals but only 17 percent of C-suite executives. They blame this gap on the pervasiveness of gender stereotypes, which lead to a kind of 'benevolent sexism' that's as damaging as it is unintentional. Kramer and Harris acknowledge that systemic change is important, but it takes time, which leaves current would-be executives in the dust. The authors discuss managing perceptions, being aware of body language, crafting communications, and using anger to its best effect...a well-organized, well-thought-out call to action..." —*Publishers Weekly*

"*Breaking Through Bias* teaches women strategies they can use to counteract the negative effect of gender biases, while showing men what actions they can take to help advance their women colleagues. This book deserves widespread attention!"

—**Hon. Jessica A. O'Brien**, President, Women's
Bar Association of Illinois

"Women are more qualified, educated, and prepared for leadership roles in every field—business, law, politics, and technology—than ever before. Yet, well into the twenty-first century, we still encounter the old barriers of prejudice and gender bias. *Breaking Through Bias* provides women with hugely impactful tools that can be put to use right now to confront gender issues and, yes, partner with enlightened men to promote our advancement."

—**Jan Schakowsky**, Congresswoman, Ninth District of Illinois

"Change cannot come fast enough in the pursuit of gender equality in the workplace. In *Breaking Through Bias*, Andie and Al provide strategies that allow women—and men—to create their own change by teaching us to communicate in a way that overcomes biases and stereotypes. This information is invaluable for all professionals looking to accelerate within inclusive workplaces around the globe."

—**Deborah Gillis**, President & CEO, Catalyst

"It is exciting to see the ideas that Andie has been using for so long to personally mentor women now being made available on a broad scale in this terrific book. A great read for any woman who wants to take control of her career and be seen as the smart, capable woman she is."

—**Julie Howard**, Chairman & CEO at Navigant Consulting, Inc.

"Andie and Al tackle the all-important subject of gender-correlated communication styles in the workplace from a fresh perspective. Combining their own real-life experiences (as a woman and as a man) with solid research, *Breaking Through Bias* is a highly readable book. Offering both practical advice for women and essential knowledge to the men who want to support them, this is a book to read and to share with others."

—**Carol Frohlinger**, President, Negotiating Women, Inc.

"Barriers to gender equality persist. This groundbreaking book encourages talented women to persevere on the road to achieving the success they seek. This book should be mandatory reading for women both at the onset of their careers and on the path to the top of their profession."

—**Laurel G. Bellows**, Managing Principal, The Bellows Law Group, P.C. and past President, American Bar Association

"Andie and Al have written an exceptional book—and an important one. It reflects decades of experience in thinking about how to overcome gender bias, and is chock-full of practical and accessible strategies for surmounting the challenges that women—and men—face. It should be read and studied by anyone seeking to win in the worldwide battle for talent."

—**Jeffrey E. Stone**, Chairman, McDermott Will & Emery LLP

"Andie has worked tirelessly on the advancement of women in workplaces for so many years, and the wisdom and insights from that work are elegantly captured in this book! *Breaking Through Bias* is a great resource for women navigating the realities of workplace gender bias and the men who want to make their workplaces work better for everyone! Andie and Al's advice is practical without asking women to be something other than who they are, which is why it will also be effective for those who utilize it."

—**Dr. Arin Reeves**, author of *One Size Never Fits All: Business Development Strategies for Women (And Most Men)* and *The Next IQ: The Next Generation of Intelligence for 21st Century Leaders*

"*Breaking Through Bias* serves as a wake-up call for senior business leaders. The book explores common gender stereotypes and discusses the discriminatory bias that result. Based on my own work on culture change over the past five years, I am convinced that bias in the workplace is real. Things aren't equal. I can't allow myself to be satisfied with an environment where female employees have to expend energy combatting bias, so culture change is necessary—but it is slow work. This book offers insights and practical approaches to help women manage the environment as it exists. It is essential reading for modern businesspeople of either gender."

—**Lee Richard Tschanz**, Vice President North America, Sales, Services, and Solutions, Rockwell Automation

"The medical profession is no more free of gender bias than all other professions that make up our economy. From the early stages of training to achieving the attending physician status, bias exists at every level. Thus, I am enthusiastically recommending that women medical students, residents, and fellow colleagues read and reread *Breaking Through Bias*."

—**Neelum T. Aggarwal, MD**, Chief Diversity Officer of American Medical Women's Association; Chair of Mentors, Advisors and Peers Committee, Women in Bio (Chicago); Associate Professor, Departments of Neurological Sciences and Rush Alzheimer's Disease Center

"Andie and Al have created the perfect primer to navigate through the treacherous waters of gender bias. This is not a book you read and donate to your neighborhood library! You'll want to keep it handy for its many insights and apply them to the countless scenarios that emerge throughout your personal and professional life. This is the book I wish I had more than thirty-five years ago when I launched my career in public relations."

—**Cheryl Procter-Rogers**, PR strategist and executive coach,
A Step Ahead PR Consulting and Coaching

BREAKING THROUGH BIAS

COMMUNICATION
TECHNIQUES
for **WOMEN** *to*
SUCCEED *at* **WORK**

ANDREA S. KRAMER
ALTON B. HARRIS

First published by Bibliomotion, Inc.
39 Harvard Street
Brookline, MA 02445
Tel: 617-934-2427
www.bibliomotion.com

Printed in the United States of America
Image credit: page 137. Reproduced with permission of Punch Ltd., www.punch.co.uk

Library of Congress Cataloging-in-Publication Data

Names: Kramer, Andrea S., author. | Harris, Alton B., author.
Title: Breaking through bias : communication techniques for women to succeed
    at work / Andrea S. Kramer and Alton B. Harris.
Description: Brookline, MA : Bibliomotion, Inc., [2016] | Includes
    bibliographical references and index.
Identifiers: LCCN 2015040059 | ISBN 9781629561042 (hardcover : alk. paper) |
    ISBN 9781629561059 (ebook) | ISBN 9781629561066 (enhanced ebook)
Subjects: LCSH: Communication in management—Sex differences. | Communication
    in organizations—Sex differences. | Women—Communication. | Sex
    discrimination. | Stereotypes (Social psychology) | Vocational guidance
    for women.
Classification: LCC HD30.3 .K695 2016 | DDC 650.101/4—dc23
LC record available at http://lccn.loc.gov/2015040059

*For Cynthia and the brilliant, fulfilling,
and productive life she has ahead of her.*

CONTENTS

PART IV
Communicating in Difficult Situations

ANDIE'S PREFACE

When I graduated from law school, I was fortunate to have a number of job offers, but two in particular interested me. One was from a large, well-known, and highly prestigious law firm; the other was from a small, three-year-old firm with only seven lawyers, hardly any reputation, and no national prestige. The large firm promised me a place in a prominent, nationally recognized tax department, the opportunity to earn a great deal of money, and immediate personal and professional status. The small firm said it would give me whatever resources and support I needed and send me to whatever classes I thought would be useful. But at the small firm I would be the only tax lawyer, and although the partners had great hope for the future, they made it clear that the firm's prospects were not certain. I was young, undoubtedly foolish, and certainly without fear of failure, so I accepted the small firm's job offer.

The decision was right for me. I spent almost fifteen years at that firm. And two things are most memorable. First, the firm kept all of its promises to me, and I learned how to be a real lawyer. I became a partner, brought in my own clients, and chaired the firm's tax group, which included seven lawyers by the time I left.

Second, and much more importantly, my being a woman had nothing to do with my professional development or advancement. I worked with a group of senior lawyers, all of whom were men, not one of whom, not once, not even for an instant, made me feel that my being a woman made a whit of difference to my becoming a great lawyer. Growing as a lawyer is never smooth sailing, but my being a woman was never the cause of the rough waters I encountered.

Because of the opportunities that firm gave me, the time came when I needed the resources of a much bigger law firm to meet the needs of my clients. When I left, I was apprehensive. I expected many differences, but the most disturbing one I encountered was the one I least expected: gender bias. At my new firm—and at all of the other very large law firms with which I was now dealing—I saw obstacles in women's career paths that were not in the men's. I encountered inconsistencies in the opportunities made available to women and men. And I found unfair demands placed on fabulous women trying to become good lawyers and raise children. It all reminded me of the career advice I received in my teens. I was told there is a difference between being a "lawyer" and a "lady lawyer." Lawyers could be successful and happy; lady lawyers could never be both. Well, I was a lawyer, a successful one at that, I was a lady, and I was happy. I knew that other women could be just as successful and happy as I was, and I would be damned if I was going to sit back and watch law firms and other professional and business organizations discriminate against these women, force them to choose between success and happiness, or make it far less likely that they would attain successful, satisfying careers than their male colleagues.

Coming face to face with the reality of gender bias after not seeing it at the start of my career taught me several things. First, I learned that there are truly gender-neutral workplaces, but these are a precious few. By and large, we live in a society in which men make the decisions about career advancement, and those decisions are often affected by gender stereotypes (conscious and unconscious). Second, I learned that if women are going to advance as they aspire to—and all of the research shows that young women are just as ambitious as young men, if not more so—then they cannot passively accept the current gender-skewed state of affairs. Women need to recognize and purposefully counter the gender stereotypes and biases present in many workplaces. Third, I realized that successful women deal with gender stereotypes through nuanced and carefully honed communication techniques.

More than twenty years ago I made a commitment to myself to do everything in my power to help other women be successful *and* happy in their careers—to come as close as possible to experiencing the gender-neutral career path I had been lucky enough to follow when I started my career. I have been trying to make good on that commitment ever since.

In the early 2000s, I began to speak publicly about how women can best confront the difficulties they face advancing in their careers because of gender bias. During the past ten years I have spoken on this topic before more than one hundred groups, including the Professional Golfers' Association of America, the National Court Reporters Association, the YWCA, the Farm Credit Administration, the Association of Latino Professionals in Finance and Accounting, and the League of Black Women. I have written numerous articles and guides, and led dozens of workshops aimed at helping women advance in their careers.[1] In 2005, I cofounded the Women's Leadership and Mentoring Alliance (WLMA), a not-for-profit corporation, of which I am the current board chair. WLMA provides a national mentorship program for women in multiple industries and professions. Most recently, I developed a leadership institute for the Women's Bar Association of Illinois.

As my work began to attract national attention, I realized that my communication techniques for overcoming gender stereotypes and bias had struck a chord with women across America. As a result, I decided to write this book to reach even more women. But I knew I couldn't write it on my own. My husband, Al, and I have been discussing ways to cope with gender stereotypes and biases for decades and recently started to write together on the topic. We have both sadly watched the disparity in the career achievements of women and men grow larger than it was in the mid-1990s. As we discussed the shape and content of a book on gender communication, it became clear to me that a male perspective would be invaluable and provide a unique addition to my views. By combining our experience and perspectives with stories from women we have coached and mentored, as well as with recent social science research, we are able to provide women and men with a clearer understanding of the operation of gender stereotypes and bias. Together we offer helpful and immediately actionable advice about how to communicate to avoid or overcome the career-disrupting effects of stereotypes and bias. Al and I both believe that women can take control of their own careers and achieve the success and satisfaction that they desire and to which they are entitled. With this book, women have the tools to prevent gender bias from preventing them from going as far and as fast in their careers as their talents will allow them.

Andrea S. Kramer
Chicago, IL

AL'S PREFACE

I am a founding partner of that small law firm where Andie started her legal career. I am proud of our gender-blind environment, which allowed her to develop into the superb lawyer she is today. But Andie's story is not the whole story. During our firm's forty-year history, we did encounter situations involving gender bias. When we did, we responded with a single objective: to make our workplace fair and free of discriminatory treatment of anyone by anyone. Our firm has now merged with a much larger firm, but before we did in early 2015, I believe we offered women career advancement opportunities second to none: varied, substantive, and gender neutral.

Yet despite these efforts, the disparities in women's and men's longevity at the firm and their eventual career achievements were striking: we hired women and men in almost equal number but we lost far more women than men, and a mere 10 percent of our equity partners were women. Why did this happen? Most certainly not because our female lawyers lacked talent or ambition. They were without exception bright, enthusiastic, and committed to becoming successful lawyers. But something was missing in many of their preparations for high-pressure, high-expectation, high-competition careers. Too many of these women—and too many women generally—are unprepared to compete for career advancement with and against their male counterparts. Too many of these fabulously talented women left our firm because they felt frustrated by their lack of tangible career success: no clients of their own, no clients of anyone else's asking specifically to work with them, no senior female role models for them to emulate. Too many of our women went on maternity leave and chose not to come back. I have counseled, cajoled, and begged many of these women to stick with their careers, but I have seldom been successful. Neither my firm nor the practice of law is unique in this regard. I have represented hundreds of clients over the course of my career. At many of these businesses, I worked with enormously talented senior women who were involved at the start of a project but gone before it was finished.

The low percentage of women in senior leadership positions in the United States is undoubtedly due to many factors, but I am convinced the principal one is that senior leaders controlling women's career advancement—almost all of whom are men—generally hold a set of gender stereotypes that heavily handicap women. Most women working for these men simply do not know how to cope with these stereotypes. As a result, without any conscious or malicious intent on anyone's part, these stereotypes operate to create severe roadblocks in women's career paths. It is unlikely that in the near term anything can be done to eliminate these stereotypes from the workplace, but as a result of working with Andie and many other talented women who have been able to deal successfully with stereotype bias, I have come to believe that women themselves can do a great deal to avoid or overcome the discriminatory consequences of these stereotypes. I am convinced that with the right information and training, ambitious, talented women can go very far on their own toward ending the shameful disparity in women's and men's career achievements. Women do not need to wait for our gender-biased workplaces to be transformed into gender-neutral workplaces. Or to start acting more like men. With the right encouragement and preparation, I believe women can claim their seats at the leadership table and speak with voices that will be heard.

That brings me to the reasons I am writing this book with Andie. First, high-potential, once-eager women often drop out of their careers or opt for less intense, less interesting, and less financially rewarding positions because they find their professional lives to be unfulfilling, frustrating, or oppressive. I believe this is the result of the stereotype-driven dynamics of their interpersonal relationships with their male colleagues and supervisors. Many women are simply not prepared to deal effectively with those dynamics. But I believe that with sufficient information about gender stereotypes and with concrete, practical advice about how to cope with them, women can achieve full and satisfying careers.

In writing this book with Andie, I hope to help talented and ambitious women change their own interpersonal gender dynamics in a way that makes their careers more fulfilling and less frustrating and discouraging. I am near the end of my legal career, but before it ends, I want to see more female equity partners in my new law firm and more women in leadership positions in all American industries. I think that this book is an important step in that direction.

The second reason I am writing this book is that women can benefit from a male perspective on gender stereotypes and the use of communication techniques to overcome their adverse consequences. Andie and I share similar perspectives on these issues, but our views are not identical. It is my hope that by bringing our perspectives together, women will gain a clearer picture of how the workplace looks from both a female and a male perspective. Moreover, I hope that our dual perspectives will provide women with original, practical, and effective advice that will aid their career advancement.

My third reason for writing this book is that most senior men don't have a clue about how much harder it is for a woman to succeed in a career than it is for a man. Too many of these men don't think about unconscious gender bias at all, or they do not take the issue sufficiently seriously. This book is obviously for women: it is addressed to women, talks about problems that are unique to women, and offers communication strategies and techniques tailored specifically for women. But I believe that men—particularly men in senior leadership positions— need to read this book as well. They need to read it to understand why women find it so tough to advance in their careers. They need to read it to learn how to recognize and address gender bias in their personal and professional interactions. Finally, they need to read this book so they will become motivated to offer a helping hand to the women with whom they work. Senior men need to mentor and sponsor more women. They need to make sure the women who work for them are challenged, criticized, trained, encouraged, compensated, and promoted to the same extent that men are. My hope is that, because a man is one of the authors of this book, other men will read it and recognize the need to focus on fostering women leaders in their own organizations.

The fourth and final reason I am writing this book is for our daughter. She is an incredibly talented, ambitious, and personable young woman who believes the world is a meritocracy, that women and men are equal not only in their abilities but also their opportunities, and that nothing will hold her back in her future medical career except her own shortcomings and mistakes. This book is in part my gift to her. It contains the advice I will want to give her when she finds that the world is not a meritocracy, that women's and men's career opportunities are not the same, and that her career can be impeded for reasons that have nothing to do with her talent but everything to do with her being a woman.

Alton B. Harris
Chicago, IL

INTRODUCTION

The great disparity in the number of women and men in senior leadership positions in the United States is a striking testament to just how much harder it is for women to advance in a career than it is for men. Women make up 45 percent of entry-level professionals in the U.S., but as they move up the career ladder, women are severely underrepresented at every level, with the disparity greatest in senior leadership. Women are 37 percent of managers, 32 percent of senior managers, 27 percent of vice presidents, 23 percent of senior vice presidents, and only 17 percent of C-suite executives.[1] At 47 percent of the highest-earning public companies in Silicon Valley, there is not a single female executive. Women hold only 16 percent of the director seats at S&P 1500 companies, and only 2 percent of financial services industry CEOs are women.[2] At S&P 500 companies, women make up 45 percent of the workforce, but only 25 percent of senior-level executives and only 5 percent of the CEOs.[3]

Women make up 45 percent of law firm associates but only 17 percent of equity partners.[4] Thirty-six percent of all physicians are women, but only 16 percent are deans of medical schools.[5] At colleges and universities, women hold only 30 percent of full professorships, and at these institutions only 26 percent of the presidents are women.[6]

Looking at the top-grossing American movies in 2014, women made up only 7 percent of the directors, producers, writers, cinematographers, and editors.[7] In American government, only 12 percent of state governors are women, only 17 percent of the mayors in the largest 100 cities are women, and only 19 percent of the United States House and Senate are women.[8]

Many more similar statistics are available, but the point should be clear enough: women just aren't as "successful" in the business, professional, academic, entertainment, and governmental worlds as are men. The explanations commonly offered for this gap in gender achievement are all over the map: differences in the ways girls and boys are raised as children, treated in school, and coached in athletics; social mores, workplace demands, and domestic expectations; and legal policies and conventions. Undoubtedly, all of these factors and more play a role in the career achievement gap, but the primary cause—with no close second—are the stereotypes that the people who control the checkpoints and gatehouses on women's and men's career paths hold about women, men, work, leadership, and the family. These stereotypes foster discriminatory biases that seriously hamper women's career progress. Yet because these stereotypes are largely unconscious, the biases that result from them operate for the most part without the awareness of either the gatekeepers or the women whose careers are adversely affected by them.

This book is addressed to women (we'll get to men in a moment) who do not want their careers to stall or derail simply because they are women. More importantly, this book is an extended argument that women can prevent this from happening without waiting for large-scale structural or organizational changes in workplace practices.

THE PERVASIVENESS AND CONSEQUENCES OF GENDER STEREOTYPES

Many people, perhaps most people, believe women and men are different. Not just different biologically, but fundamentally different in their orientations toward the world. Although there are sharp disagreements about the reasons for this difference, people generally think women are communal, men are agentic; women gentle, men aggressive; women caregivers, men providers. If such views about the differences between women and men accurately reflected reality, the disparities in their leadership achievement would make perfect sense. If women are cooperative and warm but not ambitious and decisive, if they are friendly and kind but lack competence and leadership ability, and if they are caring and compassionate but not committed or competitive, women *should* earn less than men, reach the C-suite, equity partnership, and academic tenure less often than men, drop out of high-potential careers at a higher rate than men, and spend more time doing domestic tasks than men.

The problem with this "women and men are just different" view is that there is no empirical evidence that this is the cause of the persistent achievement gap between women and men. Indeed, the available evidence points in the opposite direction. But whether or not women's and men's "natures" are different, shouldn't we still be focusing all of our attention and energy on legal and institutional reforms that will make American workplaces fairer and less biased against women? Of course, *someone* should, and there are many sensible and persuasive advocates for needed workplace changes.[9] The problem with this "fix the system" approach is that we see no hope that any of these reform proposals will be implemented within a time frame that will meaningfully change women's immediate prospects for career success. And it is women's career prospects *today* with which we are concerned. Our focus, therefore, is neither on women's and men's "natures" nor on fundamental system-wide reforms, but rather on what women can do for themselves to make their own careers more successful, satisfying, and sustainable *right now*. This means paying close attention to the people who maintain the checkpoints and gatehouses on women's career paths and the stereotypes with which these people operate.

Trying to eliminate these gatekeepers' stereotypes would be difficult if not futile. But changing women's understanding of the way they should communicate with these gatekeepers should be easy. And once they have made this change, women will be able to communicate in ways that provide them with a far greater chance of achieving the sort of career success they desire. The changes in understanding and behavior we are suggesting have nothing to do with women starting to act more like men. We believe women's attitudes, abilities, and behavior are just fine the way they are and are as suitable for the boardroom as they are for the nursery. But—and this is the premise of this book—by understanding how to become better attuned to gender stereotypes, anticipating the biases these stereotypes foster, and managing their impressions, women can take control of their careers and advance on a basis comparable to that of the men with whom they compete.

Many "self-help" books for women essentially argue that women are responsible for their failure to compete successfully with men because of the way they speak or communicate. In other words, they argue that women are holding themselves back because of their speech patterns. They argue that women are too unassertive or too aggressive. Either way, they argue that women need to be "fixed" in order to succeed in their careers.

We want to be very clear from the outset that we don't think women need to be "fixed." We agree with linguist Cecilia Ford that a negative response to a woman when she speaks is "based first and foremost on the fact that she is speaking from a woman's body: speaking not 'like' a woman but 'as' a woman... [she is] penalized because she is *speaking while being a woman.*"[10] The problem, in other words, is not the way that you speak but that you are a woman speaking. And the reason *this* is a problem is because of the stereotypes that the people to whom you speak have about women and "appropriate" gender roles. The objective, therefore, is not to "fix" yourself so you can communicate "like" someone other than whom you are. The objective is for you to acquire techniques that will allow you to use your own voice, body language, and movements to communicate in ways that will result in your being listened to because you are a competent, confident, socially sensitive leader speaking, rather than your being penalized because you are a woman speaking.

COMMUNICATION AND IMPRESSION MANAGEMENT

We call the ability to communicate in ways that avoid, dispel, or overcome gender bias "attuned gender communication." As we will lay out in this book, attuned gender communication involves four pieces. The first is the cultivation and active use of the four key attitudes you need for career success: grit, a positive perspective on your abilities, a coping sense of humor, and a confident self-image. The second is high self-awareness or self-monitoring. The third is the commitment to managing the impressions you make on the people with whom you deal in your career. And the fourth is the ability to use a variety of communication techniques to make and change the impressions you make in ways that will allow you to avoid or overcome the biases that result from the gender stereotypes that are so pervasive in workplaces.

You communicate through spoken and written words, but you also communicate with the attitudes you display, your facial expressions, gestures, postures, touches, preferred personal space, dress, punctuality, responsiveness, and so on. You communicate with every aspect of your behavior, and it is the totality of your behavior that affects everything from your first impression to your ability to lead, influence, inspire, and motivate. The heart of attuned gender communication is controlling the impressions you make as a result of the attitudes you display in your verbal and nonverbal behavior. By managing what you communicate, you manage the impressions the people with whom you are dealing have of you. This is hardly a new concept. Philosopher and historian David Hume made the point in the 1770s:

> [A]n orator addresses himself to a particular audience, and must have a regard to their particular genius, interests, opinions, passions, and prejudices; otherwise he hopes in vain to govern their resolutions, and inflame their affections. Should they ever have entertained some prepossessions against him, however unreasonable, he must not overlook this disadvantage; but, before he enters upon the subject, must endeavor to conciliate their affection, and acquire their good graces.[11]

If we put "woman in a business situation" in the place of "orator" and modernize Hume's language, we have the essence of attuned gender communication in two sentences.

OUR AUDIENCE

This book is addressed to talented, ambitious women who are prepared to compete vigorously for career advancement and don't want to be held back simply because they are women. Yet in virtually every segment of our economy—and certainly in every traditionally male segment—the playing field for career advancement is decidedly tilted against women.

Women's success depends on their being able to find ways to level this playing field. Attuned gender communication involves a series of practical, real-world communication techniques that women can use to do precisely that.

MEN

Throughout this book we consistently address our comments and advice to women. This makes perfect sense given that we are writing for women about what they can do themselves to advance their careers despite working for career gatekeepers who hold gender stereotypes that lead to discriminatory treatment. But by speaking directly to women, we don't want to suggest that this book is not relevant for men. Quite to the contrary, we believe men, particularly senior men with leadership roles in business and the professions, would benefit greatly from reading this book.

Studies have consistently shown that when men become fully aware of the extent of discriminatory gender bias, they believe that gender equality for women is an important issue. Unfortunately, however, most men are simply unaware of or unconcerned about gender bias.[12] Our guess is that most men's indifference to gender discrimination is because they just don't know how much harder it is for a woman to advance in a career than it is for a man. Most men believe that they have no biases against women and that the organizations in which they work treat women and men equally. If senior-level men read this book, they will realize that neither of these beliefs is correct. And when they come to this realization, we hope they will become advocates for gender equity and valuable allies in the effort to establish gender-neutral career advancement standards. We also hope men will start to mentor and sponsor women, call out their male colleagues who behave in biased and exclusionary ways, and support initiatives to assure that women get a fair shot at getting to the top.

We have written this book the way we have because we think most of the work to be done in achieving gender parity in today's workplaces must be done by women themselves. But the more men are aware of how much work needs to be done, why it is so important, and just how hard it is, the easier it will be for women to succeed.

WHAT IS TO FOLLOW

This book is divided into four parts. In part 1, "Understanding Gender Stereotypes," we lay out the common gender stereotypes that men—and women—have about women, men, families, career, and leadership. We explain why these stereotypes are at the root of the disparity in career achievement between women and men. We discuss how these stereotypes operate as scripts for discriminatory behavior. We explore why women so often think about themselves, their careers, and their families in terms of these stereotypes. And we explain why women who "buy into" these stereotypes become uncertain, begin to doubt themselves, and accept career-limiting roles.

In part 2, "Conversations with Yourself," we address the conversations you, as a woman, need to have with yourself about your career. These are conversations about your key career attitudes—grit, mindset, humor, and self-image—and the importance of managing the impressions you make as you interact with others. These are conversations about how you, like Hume's orator, can win the "affection" of the people with whom you are dealing and "acquire their good graces."

Part 3, "Conversations with Others," is about how you should communicate—in the broadest possible sense—with the people with whom you deal in the course of your work life. Your communication in this context should have as its objective to make an impression of competence, confidence, and social sensitivity, and to avoid making an impression that triggers or reinforces hurtful gender stereotypes. We present a variety of techniques you can use to accomplish this objective. These techniques will allow you to either conform to traditional gender stereotypes or violate them. In doing one or the other or both, your goal is to deal with what is commonly called the "double bind," and what we frequently refer to as the Goldilocks Dilemma; that is, displaying traits of a strong leader that cause you to be seen as strident and unlikable, or displaying traits of a traditional "feminine" woman that cause you to be seen as lacking competence and leadership potential. Attuned gender communication is a technique women can use so that they, like Goldilocks, can avoid what is too hard or too soft, but find what is just right.

In part 4, "Communicating in Difficult Situations," we examine how you can effectively advocate for yourself without running afoul of the common expectation that women should be modest and not self-promoting. We end with a chapter focused on the key choices in your life away from work that play a critical role in your ability to maintain the commitment to your career that is essential to success. We discuss why "work–life balance" and "having it all" are gender stereotypes that do not help you achieve satisfaction either in your career or in the rest of your life. And, we explain the importance of sensibly choosing what it is that you actually want to have in your life.

Before we get to part 1, following is a glossary of the key words and phrases we use throughout this book. We hope this glossary provides a useful reference tool as you proceed through the book.

KEY WORDS AND PHRASES

Words and phrases that are used throughout the book as shorthand for more complex concepts follow.

- **Agentic:** An adjective derived from "agency"; a person with agentic characteristics exhibits stereotypically masculine traits, such as being aggressive, assertive, competitive, independent, self-confident, proactive, strong, forceful, loud, stable, unemotional, and risk taking.

- **Attuned gender communication:** A phrase we have coined to refer to an integrated series of steps to avoid or overcome career biases you face as a woman because of the gender stereotypes operating in your workplace. The steps include maintaining and strengthening the right attitudes—grit, a positive perspective on your abilities, a coping sense of humor, and a confident attitude about your power and potential; high self-awareness or self-monitoring; a commitment to managing the impressions you make; and the ability to communicate—to use the totality of your verbal, nonverbal, and written behavior—to maintain or change the impressions you make.

- **Backlash:** A catchall term that refers to the negative consequences women often experience when they act in agentic ways. These negative consequences include being excluded from important meetings, networks, and events; stigmatized as hostile, cold, bossy, unpleasant, a bitch, overbearing, and difficult to work with; criticized for lacking in social sensitivity, warmth, and likability; discriminated against with lower pay, fewer promotions, and fewer job opportunities; and rendered ineffective by having contributions, ideas, and leadership potential ignored.

- **Benevolent bias:** An attitude often expressed by senior men who believe that traditional gender stereotypes correctly characterize women's capacities and appropriate roles. As a consequence, these men behave in an apparently benevolent way toward the women who work for them—solicitous, kind, considerate, concerned, helpful, protective, and patronizing—but they do not provide these women with the same career opportunities and responsibilities as men. It is a form of subtle sexism.

■ **Bias:** A generally unconscious attitude that people in one stereotype classification are better or preferable to people in another classification. This attitude can be manifested by advancing, providing opportunities to, and more highly compensating people in one classification rather than people in another classification even if they are equally qualified in all relevant respects. Bias can also be demonstrated by not providing opportunities, resources, and assistance to people in one classification that are provided to people in another classification even if they are no more qualified or entitled in a relevant respect.

■ **Communal:** An adjective derived from "community"; a person with communal characteristics exhibits stereotypically feminine traits, such as being nurturing, kind, sympathetic, concerned with the needs of others, socially sensitive, warm, approachable, understanding, solicitous of others' feelings, concerned about maintaining cordial relationships, emotional, sentimental, gentle, domestic, family focused, good with children, modest, and friendly. Such a person is usually seen as an aide but not a leader.

■ **Double bind:** A situation in which a woman suffers adverse career consequences whichever way she behaves: if she is communal she is likable but not regarded as a leader; if she is agentic she is competent but regarded as not likable and subject to backlash. We often refer to this situation as the Goldilocks Dilemma: appearing too tough or too soft but rarely just right.

■ **Feminine stereotypes:** The traditional, often unconscious, belief that women are and should be communal, and should not be (very) agentic.

■ **Grit:** An attitude of high tenacity: a dedication to pursuing, with energy and focus, a long-term goal despite failure, adversity, and plateaus of progress.

■ **Impression management:** A person's conscious effort to behave—to communicate—in ways designed to shape or change the impressions other people have of her or him.

■ **Masculine stereotypes:** The traditional, often unconscious, assumption that men are and should be agentic and that they should not need to be (very) communal.

■ **Mind priming:** A technique for conditioning or focusing your mind so that you behave in more positive, forceful, and confident ways. This basic technique involves spending five minutes writing about a time when you felt particularly powerful or happy. Mind priming is a technique to be used before a significant career event, such as a job interview, speech, important meeting, negotiation, or sales pitch.

■ **Power posing:** A technique for using your body posture to positively affect your self-image. Posing in a high-power position such as the Wonder Woman position or the runner's victory stance for two minutes increases your testosterone and reduces your cortisol, thereby improving your confidence and reducing your anxiety.

■ **Self-monitoring:** A state of acute self-awareness of the impressions you are making on the people with whom you are dealing. This awareness allows you to modify your behavior—your communication—to make the impression the situation calls for. Someone who is poor at self-monitoring is not influenced by the communication cues from others, choosing to remain "herself" no matter what the situation.

■ **Stereotypes:** Unconscious mental mechanisms that we use to classify people and then ascribe characteristics to all members of these classes. The characteristics thus ascribed to particular people have no validity or basis in reality. These classifications all function as scripts for how we should relate to people in these stereotype categories. Although some stereotypes are benign, others, such as the gender stereotypes, lead to highly discriminatory behavior.

■ **Stereotype threat:** A psychological state in which a person's performance is inhibited or impaired because she (or he) is aware that particular tasks have a strong association with a specific social group of which she (or he) is not a member; for example, women's performance on mathematics tests may be impaired by the negative stereotype that women have weaker math ability than men.

PART I

Understanding Gender Stereotypes

1

The Elephant in the Room

A great deal of attention is now being paid to workplace practices and the burdens they impose on women, particularly women with small children. The assumption seems to be that if only American workplaces did not demand so much "face time," encouraged more flextime, allowed telecommuting, provided generous maternity leaves, and created welcoming reentry programs, women would be able to advance in their careers in a manner comparable to men.

Unfortunately, as sensible as these (and other) workplace changes would be, we seriously doubt they would do much to end the disparity in women's and men's career achievements. The reason is that none of these changes gets at the real cause of women's and men's disparate career experiences. The elephant in the room of gender career achievement, so to speak, is the stereotypes people controlling women's career advancement opportunities tend to hold about women, men, families, careers, and leadership. Without acknowledging and addressing the persistence of these stereotypes and the biases that result from them, women's career advancement will continue to be disrupted and blocked without regard to the changes made in workplace practices.

GENDER STEREOTYPES ARE SCRIPTS FOR DISCRIMINATORY BEHAVIOR

The stereotypes with which we are concerned are preconceived views about the characteristics of various types of people. These stereotypes act as both sorting mechanisms and behavioral guides. We use stereotypes to assign people to particular categories—friend, foe, desirable, undesirable, worthwhile, worthless, and so forth—and we then rely on these stereotypes to tell us how we "should" relate to the people in those categories. Some stereotypes are benign and can lead to harmless or even socially beneficial behavior. An example might be a belief that "Drivers who take their turn at stop signs are courteous people." Stereotypes of this sort are useful and underpin much of our productive social interactions. But other stereotypes are far from benign and are likely to lead to discriminatory behavior. An example might be "Women are poor at mathematics."

People generally believe they don't judge other people based on stereotypes and that they are free of the biases that stereotypes foster. But psychological and sociological studies make clear that virtually all of us have implicit biases against groups that are different from us (outgroups), whether those groups are defined by economic or social status, race, religion, or ethnicity, or by education, sexual orientation, or gender. Members of out-groups are often criticized, excluded, and unfairly treated. School access, housing patterns, social acceptance, political opportunity, and workplace advancement are all affected by such implicit biases.[1]

Women pursuing careers in traditionally male industries, professions, job types, and areas of economic activity are subject to particularly severe implicit biases. One recent study revealed that approximately 75 percent of people think "men" when they see career-related words such as business, profession, and work, but think "women" when they hear family-related words such as domestic, home, and household. An overwhelming majority of people associate men with leadership positions such as boss, CEO, and director, while they associate women with aide positions such as assistant, attendant, and secretary.[2] And, most people think men when they hear the words math, science, or surgeon and think woman when they hear the words nurse, caregiver, and grammar school teacher.

Such associations are certainly understandable, given that women and men do often serve in gender-differentiated roles. But as Al's following story makes clear, such stereotypes are by no means always correct, and they can have highly discriminatory consequences.

Al: On a recent flight from Chicago to Washington, D.C., an airline employee sat next to me on her way home. The weather had been terrible, flights had been cancelled over the past two days, and I was pleased my flight had boarded. The airline employee said she was flying home after having been called up at 1 a.m. for an early flight to Chicago. She was now "dead heading" back to D.C. and then to her home in Roanoke, Virginia. I thought to myself, "Why would the airline call up a flight attendant as far away from D.C. as Roanoke?" I then turned to really look at my seatmate for the first time and saw she had stripes on the sleeves of her jacket and a hat in her lap. She was a pilot.

My unconscious stereotypes had been at work: women in uniforms on airplanes are flight attendants, men in uniforms are pilots. Now, while this is undoubtedly statistically true, I had clearly incorrectly categorized this woman, in this case harmlessly. But would it have been harmless if I had been in charge of hiring airline pilots and a woman applied for the job? Would that woman have had a harder time getting my endorsement than a man would have had? I hope not, but I think about that female pilot every time I find myself about to make a categorization of a person based on gender, race, or age.

We all hold and operate with a wide variety of stereotypes. Think about your own ideas about a nurse, college president, professional athlete, investment banker, marine, or beauty pageant contestant. But as filled as our minds are with stereotypes, the stereotypes we hold about people of both sexes are unique for at least four reasons. First, when we assign a person to one sex category or the other, that's the end of the matter. (Transgender issues blur this point, but its basic thrust is still valid.) Second, we cannot choose not to assign a person to one sex or the other. Thinking about a person as either a woman or a man is not optional; we do it automatically, and there is nothing we can do about it. Third, we sort people by sex as soon as we hear or see them. We know immediately if the person is a woman or a man (and if we don't, it is likely to throw us off balance). And fourth, a person's sex cuts across all other categories. No matter what other ways we may sort people—occupation, status, personality, race, age, or something else—we also sort them by sex.

Sorting people by sex is, in itself, largely benign and probably had evolutionary value. But this sorting does not stop with the biological division of the population. Once we have sorted people by sex, we then ascribe to them certain socially constructed characteristics. And despite the enormous changes in women's activities and opportunities over the past forty years, these socially constructed gender characteristics—the gender stereotypes with which we are concerned throughout this book—have hardly changed at all. The Bem Sex Role Inventory (BSRI), developed in 1974, and an extensive 2004 study of gender stereotypes identified virtually identical characteristics associated with women and men. According to the BSRI, people expect women to be affectionate, sensitive, warm, and concerned with making others feel more at ease. Men are expected to be aggressive, competent, forceful, and independent leaders.[3] The 2004 study found that people still expect women to be affectionate, sensitive, warm, and friendly, while they still expect men to be aggressive, competent, independent, tough, and achievement oriented.[4] The stereotypes about women and men identified in 1974 and 2004 are still operative today. Men are still assumed to have traits of action, competence, and independence, often called "agentic" qualities.[5] Women, in contrast, are still assumed to have traits of sensitivity, warmth, and caregiving, often called "communal" qualities.[6]

Why are we making such a big deal about these gender stereotypes? If most people think women are warm rather than assertive and that men are aggressive rather than sensitive, what is the harm? The harm is that the traits associated with women are also associated with home and caregiving while the traits associated with men are also associated with leadership and power. When a woman is assumed to be communal simply because she is a woman, she is also assumed to be suited for stereotypically feminine jobs—nurse, teacher, or administrative assistant—and not for stereotypically masculine jobs—investment banker, line manager, or CEO. This means that women are more likely to be tracked into personnel or assistant roles seen to require warmth and a sensitivity to the needs of others, while men are more likely to be assigned to leadership roles seen to require forceful, competent, and competitive behavior.[7]

DISCRIMINATORY OPERATION OF GENDER STEREOTYPES

Gender stereotypes foster discriminatory behavior in three basic ways.

- *Descriptively,* by telling us what women and men are "like": women are communal; men are agentic.
- *Prescriptively,* by telling us what women and men "should be like": women should be communal; men should be agentic.
- *Proscriptively,* by telling us what women and men "should not be like": women should not be (too or very) agentic; men should not be (too or very) communal.

Discriminatory Behavior

Gender stereotypes result in discriminatory behavior in complex and subtle ways. We can get a clearer picture of this biased behavior by separating it into negative or hostile behavior and benevolent or kindly behavior.

Negative or Hostile Biases

When a person is operating with traditional gender stereotypes, that person almost certainly has a negative view of women's competence and suitability for high-pressure, competitive leadership tasks. A telling and troubling example is revealed in a 2012 Yale University study of the attitudes of science professors toward women's potential as future scientists.[8] The researchers surveyed a broad, nationwide sample of biology, chemistry, and physics professors, asking them to evaluate an undergraduate science student who had applied for a position as a laboratory manager. All of the professors received exactly the same materials about the applicant, except 50 percent received an application purportedly from a woman and 50 percent purportedly from a man. The professors were asked to rate the student's competence and hireability, suggest an appropriate starting salary, and indicate the amount of mentoring they would be willing to offer the student. Both the female and male professors consistently judged the female student as less competent and less suitable to be hired than an identically credentialed male student. When the professors did offer a job to the female student, they offered her a lower salary and less career mentoring than they offered the men.[9] The pervasive gender bias revealed by this study is certainly not limited to academic science.

Al: Consider the story of Kim O'Grady. O'Grady was an accomplished consultant with considerable experience and a proven track record of successful engagements. He was so confident of the strength of his résumé that when he grew dissatisfied with the firm he was working for, he quit without first having another job lined up. When he started his job search, he was baffled that he was not getting any interviews, that is, until he added "Mr." before his name. After making this simple change he quickly landed a new job. He wrote about his experience in a Tumblr blog post, "How I Discovered Gender Discrimination," that has now gone viral.

Because of the gender stereotypes they hold, career gatekeepers tend to have low expectations about women's performance capabilities and potential. As a consequence, these stereotypes operate to negatively affect women's opportunities and advancement.[10] Too frequently, the mindset of these gatekeepers is that *this* job requires *these* characteristics, and women just don't have *these* characteristics.

Never mind what a woman's actual characteristics are. If the job doesn't fit the communal stereotype, a woman might not even have the chance to demonstrate her ability to do it. In 2005, the nonprofit organization Catalyst, which has as its goal creating more inclusive workplaces, surveyed 296 senior corporate executives (168 women and 128 men).[11] Catalyst asked these executives to rate the effectiveness of women and men on ten different leadership behaviors. Both the female and male executives rated women more effective at traditionally feminine tasks, such as caretaking, while rating men more effective at traditionally masculine tasks, such as leadership.[12]

Andie: I am often told that this or that organization would gladly have more women in leadership and management positions, but it doesn't have any women qualified for these jobs. I seriously doubt this ever to be true. More likely, the leaders of these organizations don't think that "women" are qualified, and therefore have not seriously evaluated the abilities of particular women in their organizations. I know qualified women in a variety of organizations all across the country who are consistently overlooked for advancement to positions for which they are clearly qualified. What is most heartbreaking for me is to watch these women grow cynical and resigned to their current positions after management has consistently failed to recognize their ambition, talent, and capability.

One of the most ironic situations I have personally encountered involved a female general counsel who had frequently expressed a concern that too few women in her medical services company were being promoted to important, executive-level positions. A friend of mine recommended that she talk with me. I visited the company, spent several hours with her, and presented a proposal for a workshop on gender bias for her senior management team—a workshop that had proven highly successful at several other companies. After our meeting, I never heard anything further from her. I asked my friend what had happened, and he told me she decided she needed a man to head the training program because a man would be more effective than a woman in presenting the case for greater participation by women in company leadership.

(Continued)

So here was a woman who was concerned that the men in the C-suite were not promoting enough women, but who believed that only a man could make the case that more women should be advanced in her company. When I first heard this, I didn't know whether to laugh or cry. I did realize, however, that if I had ever thought that the discriminatory operation of gender stereotypes was limited to men, I had been seriously wrong.

It is tempting to think that gender stereotypes will lose much of their discriminatory force when the current crop of business, professional, and scientific leaders retires and a younger, more open-minded group replaces them. Unfortunately, a recent survey makes clear that the ascendance of the millennial generation is not likely to do much to expand women's career opportunities.[13] The survey found a significant but unexpected relationship between age and attitude toward women in the workplace.[14] Younger male participants were more biased against women than were the older participants. The older the survey participant, the more comfortable he was in seeing women in traditionally male roles.[15] Men between the ages of eighteen and thirty-four were the most hesitant about women in certain roles.[16] Fewer than half of these men were comfortable with women as U.S. senators, Fortune 500 executives, president of the United States, or engineers.[17] Given these findings, it would be a serious mistake to assume that millennials will move us closer to gender-neutral workplaces.

"Benevolent" Biases

Many women work for male supervisors who treat them in what appear to be kind and considerate ways. This benevolent behavior is often shown through frequent expressions of concern for a woman's welfare, solicitousness as to her domestic responsibilities, and "extra" assistance with her job. Undoubtedly, people of goodwill are to be valued not avoided, but too often apparently kindly attitudes mask an underlying sexism. Such attitudes often come from a sense of paternalism, an assumption women need to be protected, directed, and assisted by a man when they are in the workplace.[18]

Al: Kelly, a senior manager at a large corporation based in New York City, told me that when she was first out of college she applied to be a flight attendant working out of New York City. The male interviewer said to her, "I would worry about a nice girl like you living alone in a dangerous city like New York." She told him she was a native New Yorker, walked out of the interview, and enrolled in business school.

Supervisors with benevolently sexist attitudes often praise women highly for their performance but assign them to devalued projects. If supervisors think (consciously or unconsciously) that women are emotional, weak, and sensitive, they are likely to give them easy assignments, "protecting" them from the difficulties and struggles inherent in challenging, competitive work. This is *not* the kind of help you need.

A 2012 study of a New York law firm's performance evaluations of its associates provides a classic illustration of benevolent sexism. The researchers found that the women received more positive comments (Excellent! Stellar! Terrific!) than the men did, but only 6 percent of the women, compared with 15 percent of the men, were mentioned as potential partner material.[19]

Al: Dara, a senior IT manager at a major manufacturing company, was about to roll out a new computer system for several departments and outside vendors. As the launch date approached, she ran a series of tests and concluded the system was not ready to go live. She delayed the start-up date and explained the reasons for doing so to her boss. She was shocked when he replied that he understood she needed more time to "get comfortable" with the rollout and that he would support the delay "until she felt ready." She realized he believed she had delayed the launch because she lacked the confidence to go forward on schedule. Rather than pushing her to move forward as he might have done with a man, her boss dealt with her "sympathetically," asking frequently if she needed more help. Dara later learned that after she had delayed the launch, her supervisor started making a series of personnel changes that weakened her status and authority.

The dangers a woman faces in a benevolently sexist environment can best be understood by looking at a normal career advancement path. Moving up depends upon your professional development: acquiring the knowledge, skills, and organizational savvy to be recognized as a person of competence, confidence, and potential. The only way you can acquire these traits is to be exposed to challenging work experiences that allow—and force—you to learn, develop, and prove yourself.

A challenging work experience is difficult, stimulating, and unfamiliar. It stretches your abilities and tests your determination. Undertaking such an experience helps you gain substantive knowledge and deeper insights into the complexities of your job. Experiences of this sort also help you gain self-confidence, which in turn encourages you to seek out and volunteer for even more challenging projects in the future. Not surprisingly, the frequency, quantity, variety, and difficulty of your work experiences are highly predictive of the pace and extent of your career advancement.[20] When you are engaged in a challenging project you are in the spotlight and your supervisors are watching closely. Therefore, these sorts of projects provide you the chance to demonstrate that you are ready to move up to the next rung of the career ladder.[21]

If, instead of giving you—or forcing you to take—challenging projects, your supervisors help you with your work or protect you from this sort of experience, you will never develop the skills, resilience, and confidence you need to realize your career aspirations. If you are excluded from high-profile projects that entail extensive travel or long hours, if you are given special breaks and a bit of extra help because you are a mother, if you are criticized less than comparably situated men for the same sort of job performance, and if you are encouraged not to stay late or take on extra work, guess who will lack the experience to be seriously considered when the time comes for the next round of promotions?

Andie: More than ten years ago at my current law firm, we found that at promotion time many women did not have the same depth and breadth of experience as did the men with the same years of legal experience. As a result, the men were getting promoted and the women were not. This was an unacceptable result so we changed the

(Continued)

process by which assignments were made. Each practice group was required to identify core competencies that lawyers are expected to have by the end of each year of practice. The objective was to be sure that all lawyers received the same types of assignments and development opportunities. Senior lawyers, most of whom were men, could no longer give the plum assignments to their favored male associates while giving the grunt projects and "easy stuff" to women.

It worked! In 2014, of those lawyers promoted to income partner, more than 50 percent were women and of those promoted to capital partner, close to 30 percent were women. This is a substantial change from where we were before we started this program, and it represents a better record of promoting women than most other large law firms have. But as I keep reminding myself, the change did not come about voluntarily; it required someone to build the business case for change and a commitment on the part of senior management to actually make those changes and enforce them.

All of this should be obvious enough: to advance in your career you need to develop broad and deep career-relevant skills, and to do this you need to push yourself and be pushed by your supervisors. You need more—not fewer—challenges at work. But if you are put on a pedestal, so to speak, because you have a mild and sensitive nature, you will not be exposed to the rough and tumble competitive struggles characteristic of high-pressure executive and professional lives. Therefore, you need to be wary of supervisors and career gatekeepers who exhibit respectful, caring, concerned, and protective attitudes, or who express a solicitous concern for your personal welfare. You need to be pushed, not protected; you need to be thrown into the game, not kept safe on the sidelines. Kindness shown toward you that is not also shown toward comparably situated men is sexism, plain and simple, and its consequences are anything but benevolent.

The Goldilocks Dilemma

When a woman conforms to the most basic communal stereotypes— being warm, caring, and sensitive to others' feelings—she will probably be viewed as pleasant and likable but not particularly competent or a leader. On the other hand, if she acts contrary to these stereotypes by displaying agentic characteristics—forcefully advocating a point of view, single-mindedly pursuing a competitive objective, or exhibiting a fierce commitment to performance excellence—she is likely to face backlash and be viewed as competent but socially insensitive, "bitter, quarrelsome, selfish, deceitful, devious, and unlikable."[22]

Andie: A personal experience might help illustrate just how difficult and insidious a problem is created by this tension between a woman's need to be both agentic and communal. When I was thirteen or fourteen, I already knew I wanted to be a lawyer. My parents had one friend who was a lawyer, so they arranged for me to have lunch with him. He spent our entire meal telling me why I didn't want to be a lawyer. He told me that there was a difference between "lawyers" and "lady lawyers." Lawyers can be happy and successful, but lady lawyers can never be both. If I became a lawyer, no one would ever love me. I would never get married. I would never have a family. I would not have any friends.

What was going on? Why would this grown man say such things to a young girl? As I look back, I think he was, in a very clumsy way, trying to alert me to the dilemma we pose for women by expecting that they will need to balance their social and professional relationships. My parents' friend saw the women lawyers he knew as having to choose between success and likability. I think he recognized that a woman who wants real career success and is willing to compete hard to achieve it runs the risk of social isolation. There are ways to avoid this result, which we discuss later in this book, but the point is that, whatever I thought of my lunch companion at the time, he was on to something and not just being a jerk.

The Goldilocks Dilemma is often referred to as a double bind, a condition that business and professional women know only too well: appearing too tough or too soft but rarely just right. We also refer to this as Too Hot/Too Cold/Rarely Just Right. Women obviously want to succeed in their careers, which generally requires them to behave agentically, but as human beings they also want, perhaps even need, to be liked, which generally depends on behaving communally.[23] But either way there can be negative consequences. Women, thus, can feel they are damned if they do and damned if they don't. As a result, women will often try to appear less agentic so that they can be seen as more communal.[24] Defensive behavior of this sort can take several forms.[25] One of the most common is illustrated by a 2011 study of women at the Harvard Business School (HBS). Women and men start their studies at HBS with essentially equal academic and career achievements. Yet despite this rough comparability, the study found that women prepared more but participated less in class than men; at graduation they received significantly fewer academic honors than did the men; and after graduation, the women reported their HBS experiences to have been far less positive than did the men.[26]

In seeking an explanation of why women and men responded to the HBS experience in such different ways, Harvard found that two principal factors were adversely affecting women during their time at the business school. First, there was an obvious clannishness on the part of male professors and students that isolated the women. HBS took immediate steps to correct this problem. But Harvard also uncovered a far subtler and more intractable problem. It found that the women were "self-editing in the classroom to manage their out-of-classroom image[s]."[27] The women felt less comfortable participating in class discussions because of the penalties they believed they would face if they violated the traditional communal stereotypes. They were consciously trying not to appear forceful or aggressive in the classroom so they would not be disliked outside of class. Here were large numbers of extraordinarily talented women holding themselves back academically because they were worried they would not be viewed positively or socially accepted if they were seen as competing "too hard." These women were trying to have it both ways: to succeed (a little less), but remain likable (a little more).

And, indeed, the behavior of the HBS women is entirely understandable if you think about how the exact same agentic behaviors are likely to be described when exhibited by a woman and a man:

- She's pushy; he's persuasive.
- She's bossy; he's a leader.

- She's a self-promoter, show off, and a braggart; he knows his own worth.
- She's abrasive; he's incisive.
- She's a harpy; he's tenacious.
- She's selfish; he's too busy to pitch in.
- She's aggressive and hostile; he's a go-getter.
- She's rude; he's direct and to the point.

Al: Dan told me about a recent board meeting at his condominium association. Tiffany, who had just been elected to the board, raised some of the same concerns Dan had raised at an earlier board meeting, although she did not know he had done so. The board president interrupted Tiffany and in a loud voice asked, "Why are you being so aggressive?" Tiffany tried to continue but the president interrupted her again, asking, "Is it your intention to come to every meeting and be so critical?"

At that point, Dan stood up and pointed out that Tiffany was only saying what he had said several meetings earlier and that her tone of voice was far less "aggressive" than the president's was. Dan stated that Tiffany was being businesslike and that it was refreshing to have a board member prepared to raise important issues in such a straightforward way. The board president asked Tiffany to continue and never again attempted to criticize her for being "aggressive."

When I think about Dan's story, I keep coming back to the fact that without Dan speaking up, it is unlikely that the board president would have backed down. A woman can always use male allies, but sometimes they are especially valuable in dealing with particularly difficult senior men.

Let's shift gears slightly and look at the Goldilocks Dilemma in another context: motherhood. Women with children face particularly severe career penalties. They are assumed to need to be available to their children at all times, and, therefore, are assumed to be less available for career demands than women without children or men (whether the men have children or not). But if women with children demonstrate that they clearly *are* fully committed to their careers, they are assumed to be bad mothers.

> *Al:* Andie and I have always both worked full time. When our daughter was growing up, we juggled our schedules so we could be home to have dinner as a family every night we were not traveling. In order to be able to spend evenings and weekends with her, we worked at home most evenings after she had gone to bed. And one of us was always present at our daughter's school and sporting events.
>
> When our daughter was about eight years old, she came home from a friend's house and told us that her friend's mother had asked her, "What does your dad do for a living?" Our daughter answered, "He's a lawyer." Her friend's mother responded, "That's great." Our daughter expected to then be asked, "What does your mom do for a living?" But, when she wasn't, she proudly volunteered, "My mom's a lawyer too." But she did not get the same response she had about her father. Instead, her friend's mother asked her in a very sympathetic tone, "How does it feel to be raised by a nanny?"

Women with children and a strong commitment to their careers are presumed to be less warm, less likable, and more hostile than similarly committed women without children. Because of this stereotype, working mothers often face an organizational backlash: they are less likely to be hired and more likely to be offered lower salaries than their childless female coworkers, despite being acknowledged to be equally competent.[28] Indeed, one well-known 2005 study found that mothers were 79 percent less likely to be hired, 100 percent less likely to be promoted, offered an average of $11,000 less in salary, and held to higher performance and punctuality standards than women without children.[29]

> *Andie:* When I joined my current law firm, our daughter was two years old. Shortly after I got there, I mentioned something in passing about her to a partner I was working with. After that, he started

(Continued)

leaving voicemail messages asking in a condescending tone whether I could talk about our project at 5 p.m.—if I'd "still be around." I never made myself available at 5:00, but I always offered to talk to him that same night any time after 6 p.m., or to meet with him any time after 6 a.m. the next morning. He never took me up on any of my suggested meeting times. He wasn't interested in meeting, only in showing his commitment and what he assumed was my lack of it. When it became apparent to him that I was committed to both my child and my career, he stopped asking to talk at 5 p.m. Many years later, I mentioned this experience to him in the context of a gender diversity discussion. He told me that this never would have happened if he had known at the time how hard I worked. Because I was a mother, he had assumed I was not committed to my career. He was just doing his job of "identifying uncommitted members of the project team."

Having a career and raising children at the same time requires resources, assistance, and careful planning under the best of circumstances. We discuss dealing with these challenges in chapter 10, "Work and the Rest of Your Life." The point we want to make here is that working mothers, and particularly mothers who are stereotypically seen as working by "choice"—women who have successful working husbands—not only must perform a high-wire juggling act to raise their children *and* advance in their careers, but they must find ways to cope with the biases that result from the stereotypes about mothers with careers.

KEY TAKEAWAYS

■ Figure out your own biases. Before you can effectively cope with other people's gender stereotypes, you need to know your own. Take the Implicit Association Test (IAT) at Harvard University's Project Implicit webpage: https://implicit.harvard.edu/implicit/.

■ You should also learn the extent of your feminine and masculine traits by taking the Bem Sex Role Inventory test at http://garote.bdmonkeys.net/bsri.html. The results will show the relative strengths of your communal and agentic traits—and which ones you will need to strengthen—because both sets of traits are important in advancing in your career.

■ Be on the lookout for benevolent sexism. Solicitous and patronizing behavior can be just as hurtful to your career as overt negative bias. Demand challenging assignments; refuse special help or privileges; and if your male colleagues are traveling or working late, you should be traveling and working late too.

■ Likability is important, and as we stress throughout this book; you need to develop attuned gender communication skills that encourage it. But likability can be highly overrated. There are great advantages if the people you work with like you, but if they don't, that's not the end of the world, much less your career.

2

The Apple in the Room

The stereotypes that career gatekeepers have about women, men, and work often operate to discriminate against women as they pursue career advancement. As a result, the primary concern of this book is with communication techniques you can use to avoid or overcome this sort of discrimination. But women also hold stereotypes about themselves: their talents, capacities, resources, and appropriate objectives and activities. Because of these stereotypes, women *choose* "gender appropriate" college majors, jobs, and assignments; *choose* to take on a greater share of family and domestic responsibilities than their male partners; and *choose* to accept career-limiting gender roles in their workplaces. The stereotypes women hold about themselves and other women can also affect the ways in which women interact with other women at work.

We call this chapter "The Apple in the Room" because traditional gender stereotypes pose a temptation for many women:

- "I am a woman, so I am not good at math, not suited for high-pressure consulting work, and not able successfully to negotiate against men."
- "I am a woman, so I will be happier working part time and putting my family responsibilities ahead of my job."
- "I am a woman, so I need to be caring, sympathetic, and modest, not forceful, assertive, and self-promoting."

We can hear many of you saying, "Nonsense," in response to these statements. And, of course, you would be right if you are thinking traditional gender stereotypes don't reflect reality. But you would be wrong if you think that women are not tempted to accept them. These stereotypes are tempting because conforming to them promises less conflict, less frustration, and less disappointment than openly violating them. We have known far too many women who have been their own worst enemies because they believed that as women they were not able to do X or were supposed to do Y, when a comparably situated man would believe no such thing.

STEREOTYPE THREAT

When you choose to avoid a task because you believe (consciously or unconsciously) that your gender prevents you from performing that task well, you are reacting to what is often referred to as stereotype threat. When you become anxious, uncomfortable, or uncertain about your ability to perform up to your capabilities in situations in which your gender is highly salient, that is stereotype threat. And when you fear you will perform poorly at tasks that are closely associated with male stereotypes, that is also stereotype threat.

Three basic stereotype threat situations often prevent a woman from playing at the top of her game. First, when a woman feels *her* performance will reflect on other women, she may become excessively concerned about failure. She may become overly anxious, which diverts her attention from the task at hand.[1]

Second, in solving problems that women are stereotypically expected not to perform well at, a woman can become excessively concerned about trying to disprove the stereotype. This can drain resources from her working memory, which impairs her ability to perform as she would like.[2]

Third, if a woman is aware of a negative stereotype regarding women's ability to perform a specific task, she may lose confidence in her ability to perform that task. Successful performance requires skill and confidence. If your self-confidence suffers, your performance suffers.[3]

In all of these situations, the key to performing well is being able to dismiss or disregard the threatening stereotype. You need to see opportunity not threat, find sharper focus not distraction, and maintain your self-confidence not succumb to self-doubt. So how can you do this?

The answer is not to *try* to dismiss the stereotypes. This can only make the situation worse by depleting the cognitive resources available to you for performing the task successfully.[4] This is not to say that trying to avoid performance impairment due to stereotype threat is pointless. Rather, you need to do it in a smarter way. One technique is suggested by a 2008 research study of women who were asked to perform a specific task at which women were not supposed to be good. Before they began, half the participants were told that their performance would not be impaired and could even be improved by the anxiety they might experience due to the stereotype concerning the task. The other half were told nothing. Women who heard the "no impairment" statement performed up to their full potential; the other women did not.[5]

The takeaway from this study is simple: in situations that pose a potential stereotype threat for you, try telling yourself that the anxiety you may experience will have nothing to do with you lacking the ability to perform that task. In other words, you need to deliver a "no impairment" message to yourself. When you can do this and believe what you are telling yourself, you transform your anxiety from an indication of self-doubt to something more akin to stage fright, a source of adrenaline and extra strength.

Another technique to use in situations that pose a stereotype threat for you is to view yourself through a non-gender lens. Don't think, "I am the only woman in this meeting," or "The men on the other side of this transaction will try to take advantage of me because I am a woman." Instead, try to think something like, "I am one of only two MBAs in this meeting," or "I am the only one involved in this transaction who has gone through a major acquisition before." In other words, in situations where gender is highly salient and stereotype threat is likely, make a concerted effort to think about your strengths, experiences, and potential rather than your gender.

A particularly effective technique for preventing stereotypes from impairing your performance is to stop thinking that your performance of a traditionally male task will reflect your true, fixed, and permanent abilities. Rather, think of your performance as an opportunity to improve your abilities through effort and challenge. Situations of stereotype threat should be seen as opportunities to grow, expand your experience, and gain confidence. Indeed, situations of stereotype threat typically involve senior male evaluators, precisely the audience before which you *need* to perform so that you can be noticed by these career gatekeepers as a person of competence, confidence, and potential.

A fourth technique for dealing with stereotype threat is to use a coping sense of humor. Humor of this sort allows you to put difficult problems, people, and situations in a much less threatening perspective and thus avoids the anxiety, confusion, uncertainty, and inhibition that so often undermine women's performance.[6]

GENDER "APPROPRIATE" BEHAVIOR

The belief that certain activities are "appropriate" for women and certain careers are not is the result of stereotype threat, pure and simple. If you believe women are good at psychology but not computer science, you are more likely to major in psychology than computer science. If you believe women are good at personal relationships but not finance, you are more likely to take a job in human resources than the treasury department. And if you believe women are not good at negotiating but are good at administrative organization, you are unlikely to volunteer for a major merger or acquisition and more likely to offer to organize a new filing system.

The entire subject of gender-appropriate activities is a highly sensitive one. Pointing out the gender segregation in college majors—85 percent of health service majors are women but only 19 percent of engineering majors are—and occupations—80 percent of social workers are women but only 15 percent of computer programmers are—can quickly be interpreted as a form of "blaming the victim." Pointing out gender segregation in careers can be taken as an attempt to hold women responsible for having lower-status and lower-paying jobs than do men.

So before we begin to discuss this subject, we want to make clear that we don't think some college majors are better than others, that some occupations are better than others, or that some career roles are better than others. There are multiple factors affecting women's decisions with respect to all of these areas, and we have no interest in making judgments about anyone's actual choices. What we do have an interest in, however, is making you aware of the segregation by gender that pervades America's college majors, occupations, and career responsibilities. We believe that if you are sensitive to this segregation, you will be less likely to place limitations and restraints on your own work-related attitudes, choices, and behavior simply because you are a woman. As we have said, we don't want you to be more like a man, but we do want you to believe and behave as though you can do anything in your career that a man can do—and do it just as well, if not better.

Forty percent of college-educated women and men would need to change their occupations to achieve gender parity across all United States occupations. This occupational gender segregation is most often attributed to "demand-side" influences, that is, employers' decisions about who they will hire and who they will make feel welcome. There is some evidence that "supply-side" factors also play a role. This means that women's and men's personal decisions about where (and at what) they want to work contribute to this segregation. Researchers from McGill University and the Wharton School of the University of Pennsylvania looked at the jobs comparably qualified women and men applied for after having attended an elite, one-year international MBA program.[7]

Their study focused on three factors influencing a person's choice of a job: how the applicant values the specific rewards offered by the job, whether the applicant identifies with the job, and whether the applicant expects an application for that job will result in a job offer. The study examined how each of these factors affected women's and men's applications to work in the fields of finance, consulting, and general management.

The researchers found no differences in the monetary and other values women and men assigned to these jobs. Nevertheless, women were far less likely to apply for jobs in finance and consulting and far more likely to apply for general management positions than were men. The researchers found this gender disparity in applications was due almost entirely to

women not "identifying" with finance jobs because of the strong masculine stereotypes associated with them or with consulting jobs because
of anticipated difficulties with "work–life balance." The researchers concluded that the low number of women in the fields of finance and consulting is largely the result of women's "gender role socialization," that is,
the stereotypes they held about themselves and particular careers. They
also concluded, however, that when a woman can overcome exception-
ally high barriers to female participation early in her career, this may
actually reduce her gendered behavior in subsequent stages of her career.[8]

Gendered behavior is behavior that is shaped or caused by gender
stereotypes. Take one well-documented phenomenon: men typically
apply for jobs when they meet 60 percent of the job criteria, but women
typically don't apply until they feel they meet 100 percent of the criteria.[9] This is gendered behavior, pure and simple, and it is due in all likelihood to stereotype threat: women's belief that they are just not as good
at particular tasks as men and, therefore, their fear that if they are not
fully qualified for the jobs for which they are applying, they are likely to
fail. This same fear too frequently causes some women to choose assignments and positions that involve less risk, lower visibility, fewer challenges, less responsibility, and less external pressure than those chosen by
their male colleagues.[10] If you are in a traditionally male work environment, there are lots of people and situations at work that will hold you
back simply because you are a woman. You are as talented, prepared,
and capable as the men, so be your own best fan and avoid the negative
thinking about yourself or what you are capable of.

BENEVOLENT SEXISM

We discussed the dangers of benevolent sexism in the last chapter, but we
did not say anything there about a woman's temptation to accept traditional female stereotypes when they are wrapped in apparent benevolence.
Praise is a good example of this sort of packaging. When you receive praise
and compliments, it is tempting not to look behind them to assess whether
they are truly warranted. More importantly, when you receive enthusiastic praise, you may not bother to think about whether your compensation

and promotion progression are consistent with what you are being told. Too many women find themselves in situations in which they receive a lot of praise but slight career advancement. If you find yourself in such a situation, it is a sure sign your supervisors think you are a nice person but not one suitable for a leadership role in your organization. If this pattern continues for any significant period of time, your skills will dull, your self-doubt will increase, and your ambition will diminish.[11]

Being "taken care of" is another example of how benevolent sexism can create a temptation for a woman to incorporate traditional gender stereotypes into her thinking about herself. In a gender-biased workplace, a woman can easily feel exposed and vulnerable. When she then receives care, attention, and protection from a "kind" male superior, she can be tempted to welcome it, put herself under his "wing," and be guided by his preferences. By praising her positive traits—her warmth, niceness, and communal attitudes—and offering her support and special dispensations, a male protector can hide the realities of gender inequality in her workplace. In other words, in a gender-biased environment, being taken care of by a powerful man can provide a woman with a sense of security and safety.

Benevolently sexist supervisors can also package traditional gender stereotypes in a tempting way by making it clear that embracing these stereotypes will enhance your subjective life satisfaction. Benevolent sexism is all about the maintenance of traditional gender roles: kind, vulnerable women and strong, protective men. This type of sexism promotes these traditional gender roles as if they are appropriate, fair, and desirable. When a woman sees her workplace in the same way, functioning fairly with balanced, complementary, but unequal gender roles, she is far more likely to find her job comfortable and less stressful than she would if she stepped out of a traditional gender role and exhibited strong agentic qualities.

The temptation to accept and enjoy benevolent sexism is very real. But the apple that is being offered is truly a poisoned fruit. If you buy your sense of psychological satisfaction at the cost of believing a discriminatory work environment is appropriate, you have also bought yourself decreased self-esteem, increased depression, and less confidence and proactivity.[12] Beware of benevolent male supervisors who want to help you manage work and family; they come bearing gifts that will not lead to an ultimately fulfilling career.

WOMEN WORKING WITH WOMEN

Another gender stereotype with which many women are tempted is the view that women find it difficult to work with other women. At Andie's workshops, a question she is frequently asked is some variation of, "Why are the women I work for so mean (critical, hostile, nasty, unhelpful) to me?" This is puzzling because it flies in the face of the empirical evidence. For example, a 2012 Catalyst study of the career experiences of female and male MBA graduates found that these graduates received more support, mentoring, and sponsorship from senior women than senior men. In addition, women were far more likely to mentor the female graduates than were the senior men. Indeed, Catalyst concluded that senior women are more likely to support other women than they are to undermine them or block their career advancement.[13]

But if the Catalyst study correctly describes the workplace reality— and we believe it does—why are the women at Andie's workshops so concerned about the problem of women working with other women? Much of this concern arises, we believe, because of the gender stereotypes women have about other women: women should be warm, caring, supportive, and sensitive to *me*. As a result of these stereotypes, when a woman works for an agentic senior woman who is decisive, critical, forceful, opinionated, and apparently uninterested in the junior woman's feelings, the junior woman is likely to view her as unlikable, difficult, or a bitch.

Andie: At a recent workshop on gender stereotypes, I mentioned that senior female leaders can be criticized by junior women for exhibiting the same sort of agentic behavior that senior men do. I pointed out that junior women often expect senior women to be kind, solicitous, and helpful—in effect, to act very much like their mothers. At this point, Tara (a junior bank officer five years out of graduate school) spoke up to say she has always found working for the men at

(Continued)

her bank far easier than working for the women. Indeed, the only person she has ever hated working for is Adrian, a woman with whom she is now forced to work closely. Tara said she dreads Adrian's assignments, characterizing Adrian as hostile, unfeeling, and unreasonable.

I asked Tara to describe for the group precisely how Adrian acted that was different from Tara's male superiors. Tara hesitated. She reflected for a minute and then said that Adrian acted much the same way as Tara's male supervisors. Tara went on to say that on reflection, she wanted Adrian to be her friend, not a distant, direct, and forceful supervisor. When I pressed her, Tara acknowledged she did not expect this same thing from the men she worked for.

As the group started to discuss this situation, several women said they had similar reactions to many of the senior women for whom they worked. One woman suggested that junior women hold senior women to different standards than senior men. The group consensus was that women often want other women to be communal: warm, understanding, and supportive of their unique situations. They don't want other women to be demanding, goal oriented, and abrupt—agentic characteristics they willingly accept in the men for whom they work.

A second stereotype women often have about senior women is that they must have gotten to where they are for reasons other than talent—tokenism, appearance, sucking up to the senior men, seductiveness, or any number of other reasons unrelated to talent. This view is the reciprocal of the preceding "my boss is a bitch" view. When a senior woman is seen as too agentic, she is a bitch, but when she is not seen as agentic enough, she is seen as unqualified for a leadership role.

A third stereotype women often have about the women for whom they work is that they are duplicitous, selfish, and concerned only about themselves. This view often arises when a senior woman praises a female subordinate for the quality of her work yet the subordinate does not see her career advancing: no salary increases, no promotions, no formal recognition. In such situations, the problem often is not that the female supervisor is disingenuous, but that she is not powerful enough to push effectively for her subordinate. If you are working for a woman who compliments your work but you don't see tangible rewards, discuss your concerns with her. Ask her about the compensation and promotion process. Ask who makes the decisions, who has meaningful input, to whom does she make *her* recommendations? You may not get what you want, but you should get a clearer picture of what you are up against—and a better appreciation of what the senior woman is up against too.

The last gender stereotype that often leads women to regard the women for whom they work negatively is that senior women are bullies. While there certainly are women bullies, only about 30 percent of workplace bullying is done by women.[14] Nevertheless, a critical, highly demanding female supervisor will often be seen as a bully when the same conduct by a man would be accepted as an effective leadership style.

There is a clear difference between a highly critical, demanding boss and a bully. A bully is not interested in getting a good result but only in humiliating, undermining, excluding, and driving other people out of the organization.

Al: I have been reading with interest the news articles about the firing of Lt. Col. Kate Germano, who had led the only all-female marine recruit battalion for about a year. When Germano took over command of the unit, she found the women in boot camp were kept separate from the male recruits and that their performance at non-strength-related skills, such as shooting, was lower than the scores of the male recruits. The Marine Corps' mindset appears to have been that female recruits should appropriately be held to lower performance standards than the men. Germano, according to the reports, was determined to change this. In her short tenure, Germano stopped many of the separate training protocols, which resulted in improved performance by the women in her unit in almost all categories. Germano was, nevertheless, fired, because of complaints of a "hostile, unprofessional, and abusive" leadership style. Her supporters claim that Germano had only been trying to make the unit better by holding the women to tougher standards and that there would have been no objection to her conduct if she had been a man.

I am certainly not in a position to say whether Germano was actually a bully, but I doubt it. A bully does not care about the good of the organization or the people who work for her, but Germano did.[15]

Being bullied by a woman puts you in a very difficult situation. If you stick up for yourself and fight back, your conflict can be seen as a cat fight, a stereotypical view of female behavior, and a confirmation that women can't work with other women. On the other hand, if you don't stick up for yourself, you can suffer adverse career consequences.

If you are being bullied, whether by a woman or a man, you need help. Go to human resources, the head of your department, or a senior person in your organization. Real bullying creates a hostile work environment; it is illegal and should be responded to in the same way you would to sexual harassment.

JUDGING YOUR CAREER SUCCESS

Another tempting stereotype for many women is the idea that your success can be measured by your progress in relation to that of other women. We all naturally compare our abilities and achievements to those of people we consider our peers.[16] But if you assume your only peers are other women, you can delude yourself into believing you are being treated fairly when you are not. According to recent research, most women are likely to acknowledge that women in general do not receive compensation and other career-related rewards comparable to that of similarly situated men, but they are also likely to deny that they personally are subject to any gender discrimination.[17] This myth of personal uniqueness—the belief that you are being treated fairly while the rest of the women in your organization are not—is perpetuated when you compare yourself only to other women. Unless you judge yourself in relation to your male counterparts, you will never really know—or have an incentive to do something about—whether you are being treated fairly.

Andie: Marie asked my advice when she learned potentially devastating news about her career progress. She is a mechanical engineer and a successful senior executive at an international consulting

(Continued)

company. Marie had been happy at work and knew her career progression compared favorably with that of other senior women. Then, she learned by chance that several men who reported directly to her were making more money than she was. She investigated and learned that two of the three women to whom she had always compared herself also had male direct reports who earned more than they did. Marie dug further and could not find a single man at her responsibility level with any direct reports who made more than the man they reported directly to. To make matters even worse, she also learned that all of the men at her responsibility level had substantially higher salaries and routinely received larger bonuses than she did.

After she told me all of this, Marie and I worked out a four-part plan of attack. First, she would request a "no-ifs-ands-or-buts" explanation from her supervisor of the pay disparity. Second, she would ask for her supervisors' written evaluations of her—something she had never received in a form she could compare with the evaluations she had given of her direct reports. Third, she would undertake a series of changes in her communication to ensure she would be perceived as more important and valuable than she obviously was perceived at present. And fourth, she would develop a focused self-evaluation to be presented at her next annual evaluation.

Marie is in the midst of implementing her plan, but she reported back that her supervisor had been surprised by her forceful demands, but complimented her on her spunk and determination. He assured Marie that the company did not want to lose her. I don't know much about her company's culture or structure, but I do know Marie. I believe she will be vigilant until she gets what she thinks is fair—or moves on to her next career opportunity.

If you are not looking at the men in your organization when you are evaluating your career progress, you need to expand your field of vision. When pursuing a career in a traditionally male area, such as manufacturing, technology, consulting, finance, law, or medicine, you are competing primarily against men. The only way you can keep score—to know if you are being compensated and advanced as the competent, confident, high-potential person you are—is to compare yourself to comparably situated men. If you don't know comparably situated men who will share compensation information with you, start cultivating some new male friends. Ask your supervisor how you are doing relative to your male peers and demand straight answers. And pay close attention to all reports of promotions and status changes, particularly to those involving men at your level.

BELIEVING WORK IS A MERITOCRACY

A final stereotype that many women find irresistible is that their organization is fair, a true meritocracy. These women assume that if they work hard, perform well in their jobs, and lean in, they will achieve the career success they are seeking. Not believing this can sap a woman's ambition, demoralize her, and lead either to cynicism or a dropped career. This means that a woman often *needs* to believe her organization is a meritocracy; if she doesn't, she might have trouble getting up in the morning to go to work.

Whether her workplace is a meritocracy poses a real dilemma for a woman. On one hand, if she believes her workplace is unfair, that hard work and high-quality output will not necessarily result in her advancement, she may very well not try as hard as she otherwise would—creating a self-fulfilling prophecy. On the other hand, if she believes her workplace is fair and that she will be rewarded on the same basis and at the same rate as a man, she is likely to blame herself when she does not receive the same rewards. The dilemma of meritocracy is that in gender-biased workplaces, you seem to lose, no matter what you believe.[18]

Institutional and structural changes are certainly needed for our workplaces to become true meritocracies. But we are skeptical about the near-term (or far-term, for that matter) likelihood of these changes being made. The issue, therefore, is how you can advance in your career despite your organization not being a true meritocracy. Simply working harder, turning out high-quality deliverables, and evidencing your strong commitment to your job are necessary to achieve this objective, but they are not sufficient. As a woman in a traditionally male field, your advancement depends on attracting the right kind of attention—attention you draw because you are a dynamic person with savvy, confidence, and competence who does not get tangled up in gender stereotypes. Getting this sort of attention requires attuned gender communication: self-monitoring, impression management, the right attitudes, and a variety of communication techniques, all of which we begin to address in the next chapter. For now, however, keep in mind that workplace meritocracy is a myth, but with the right tools, you can succeed just as though it were not.

KEY TAKEAWAYS

■ Watch out for stereotype threat and choose assignments carefully. Understand if and when stereotype threat is triggered for you and practice the techniques we suggest to avoid it. Don't hold yourself back by letting yourself think you are not as talented, prepared, and capable as the men with whom you are competing. Give yourself a "no impairment" message that your anxiety will not affect your ability to perform.

■ Think about your achievement goals. Are you pursuing jobs or assignments because they are gender "appropriate" or because they are what you dream of doing?

■ Move out of your comfort zone. Career advancement requires you to complete challenging, high-risk projects and assignments. Make sure you seek them out.

■ Take and keep taking a hard look at how your career is advancing. Ask yourself these questions from the Catalyst report, "Good Intentions, Imperfect Execution? Women Get Fewer of the 'Hot Jobs' Needed to Advance":[19]
    1. Are you aware of the size and scope of your projects relative to those of others?
    2. Are you strategically working toward getting assigned to large and visible projects?

3. Do you step forward and volunteer to take on important assignments?
4. Have you participated in a formal leadership development program? Do you need to?
5. Are you planning for your next development opportunity? Do you have a clear idea of how to get it?

■ Glowing reviews don't translate into promotions. Promotion requires you to be noticed by your supervisors as a person with the ambition, competence, and potential to perform successfully at the next level. You need to demonstrate that you have the potential to succeed if promoted, not that you can competently perform in your current position.

PART II

Conversations with Yourself

3

Managing the Impressions You Make

Your career success depends on a variety of factors, not the least of which is just plain luck. But among those factors that are within your control, the most important are social presence, organizational intelligence, political savvy, and impressive job performance. These skills are as important for a man's career success as they are for yours. But you also need skills a man does not. You need to be able to recognize the gender stereotypes operating in your work environment and be able to avoid or overcome the discriminatory biases that result from them. To do this effectively you need to understand the relation between your behavior and the impressions people form of you. You need to be able to read people's reactions to your verbal and nonverbal behavior and change that behavior if the reactions you are getting—the impressions you are making—are not the ones you want. In other words, because of gender bias, your career success depends to a great degree on your ability to manage your impressions.

THE IMPORTANCE OF IMPRESSION MANAGEMENT

Imagine a typical mixed-gender business meeting. Whatever the purpose of the meeting, the participants are likely to hold at least three stereotypes. First, they will expect the men to be agentic, that is, tough-minded, aggressive, confident, competent, independent, and assertive.

Second, they will expect the women to be communal, that is, friendly, unselfish, warm, kind, compassionate, supportive, and nurturing. And third, they will expect anyone capable of leading the meeting to be agentic. Given these stereotypes, one of two scenarios is likely to play out if one of the women at the meeting tries to exercise a leadership role. If she attempts to take charge without behaving in an agentic matter, she is likely to be ignored; but if she seeks to lead in an agentic way, she is likely to face a backlash because she is regarded as unfeminine and abrasive. No matter which approach she takes, she is likely to face negative career consequences.

An ambitious woman who encounters this sort of double bind on multiple occasions can easily come to believe that she will never be allowed to exhibit her competence and leadership potential unless the organization for which she works becomes more female friendly. And then, when this doesn't happen, she is likely to drop out of the career advancement game altogether or resign herself to a workplace reality of frustration, anger, and disappointment.

Al: After Bethany, a lawyer in another city, had read in an earlier draft of this chapter the sentence "when this doesn't happen, she is likely to drop out of the career advancement game altogether or resign herself to a workplace reality of frustration, anger, and disappointment," she sent me the following e-mail:

I circled that sentence and wrote "ME" beside it. In all of the major corporations where I have worked, younger, less experienced, not as talented men have been promoted over me. Men in power pick younger men who remind them of themselves. It takes a special man to recognize that diversity of thinking in a business and the C-suite is beneficial. But men who would like to help women are often afraid that doing so will make them look weak. It is easier for them to just keep finding "mini-me's" to promote so they don't have to deal with fallout from their male colleagues.

My current boss recently told me he was considering promoting a new hotshot male lawyer, two years out of law school with no law

(Continued)

license (he has never taken the bar exam) to be assistant general counsel because he has "the right characteristics." I expressed my concern that this young man was not nearly ready and didn't have the experience (or law license) for such a position. My boss got very angry and said to me, "I have every confidence in my ability to pick the right people to hire and promote." And of course, he has the power to do whatever he wants.

I could go on for hours, days, weeks, and years. I am just angry, bitter, and disappointed. Despite how frequently I tell myself "just do your time in Folsom Prison," I can't shut off my ambition and strong desire to succeed. But, when success doesn't come, I just get more angry and bitter. As I have gotten older, I have gotten better at just "doing my time," but when I do this, I feel I am letting down the other professional women in the organization. I just don't seem to be able to win.

Bethany's frustrated ambition and dashed dreams are heartbreaking. Unfortunately, we know of far too many women with similar stories. But we believe there is a way forward for Bethany and other women, a way for them to be seen as leaders without being seen as either pushy unlikable bitches *or* sweet but "not competent enough to move up" women.

Let's return to our example of a mixed-gender business meeting. As we pointed out, a woman at such a meeting who attempts to play a leadership role by exhibiting *exclusively* communal or agentic traits is likely to face the discriminatory consequences of the double bind. But when she is able to selectively use both sets of traits, as appropriate—in other words, when she can manage the impressions she is making—she stands a good chance of escaping or minimizing the negative consequences of being seen as either "too soft" or "too hard."[1]

We recognize that simply recommending that you use a combination of agentic and communal communication styles to avoid getting caught in a double bind is hardly helpful. It leaves unanswered a whole host of practical questions about the nature of these different communication styles, how to use them most effectively, and when they are most appropriate. The chapters that follow address these questions in considerable detail, but before we get there, we want to make clear why your ability to control your communication and hence the impressions you make is so critical for your career success.

WOMEN, IMPRESSION MANAGEMENT, AND AUTHENTICITY

Impression management is a simple concept: it is the conscious control of what and how you are communicating in an effort to shape the impressions other people have of you.[2] You are continually seeking rewards in the course of your career life: respect, recognition, opportunities, increased compensation, and advancement. If you can shape the impressions that the people who control these rewards have of you, you can also shape (to a great extent) the ways in which these people treat, evaluate, and talk about you. When you are able to control the impressions you make, you have greatly increased the likelihood that you will receive the rewards you are seeking.

There are many factors that will influence when, why, and how you seek to manage your impressions. Two key factors, however, underlie all effective impression management. The first is a high degree of self-awareness, or what the social science literature often calls high self-monitoring. This is an awareness of *what* you are communicating—not just the substantive content of what you are saying, but everything you are conveying about yourself as a result of the totality of your behavior. You are attuned to *whether* the impressions you are making as a result of your communication are the ones you want to be making. The second is an ability to use a variety of communication techniques to change the impressions you are making. In other words, effective impression management depends on both acute self-awareness and on having a facility for nuanced verbal and nonverbal behavior. Much of the remainder of this book is devoted to how you can acquire and use both these skills.

Andie: Simone is an experienced lawyer with an impressive record of achievements. She is smart and very, very intense. Simone recently assumed a new position within the legal department of the corporation for which she works. She is now the only woman participating in extensive drafting sessions in preparation for a major acquisition. Simone was not uncomfortable being the lone woman in these sessions, but she was struggling with the dynamics of her relationship with the senior man on the project.

As Simone explained the problem to me, Matt, the senior person, will listen to her ideas but then turn to Simone's colleague, Chuck, to discuss the points as if Simone were not in the room. Matt actually turns his body away from her and toward Chuck. Simone asked for my advice about how she could get Matt to interact directly with her. I have known Simone for a long time so after we talked for a while, I asked her if, perhaps, her intensity, her unrelieved focus on making her points, and her lack of friendly banter were making Matt uncomfortable. She acknowledged this was possible, but she also said, "My intensity is what has gotten me to where I am. Surely that's a positive aspect of who I am. I can't change that." I pointed out that Matt was not going to engage with her unless and until he felt comfortable doing so. If he found her intensity hard to take, she would either have to dial it down or accept the status quo. So she grudgingly said, "Okay," and we discussed a number of behavioral changes she could try that would allow her to come across as more relaxed, approachable, and engaging.

Simone got back to me the very next day in an e-mail that read: "I talked slower and tried to appear relaxed, pleasant, and interested in Matt's life away from the office. I was careful to watch Matt's reactions, and when he seemed to be getting uncomfortable I tried to lighten things up. Well, it worked; he interacted directly with me and only once tried to engage Chuck. I think I am on the right track."

Let's return to the claim that by using both communal and agentic communication styles you can effectively avoid or overcome the gender biases arising from the leadership double bind. In a recent study, researchers tracked 132 female and male MBA graduates over an eight-year period.[3] Some but by no means all of the women in this group were highly self-aware and comfortable using both agentic and communal communication techniques as appropriate. These high self-monitoring women received 1.5 times as many promotions as agentic men; 1.5 times as many promotions as communal women; 2 times as many promotions as communal men; and 3 times as many promotions as agentic women.[4]

The results of this study provide a strong argument for why women should manage their impressions through a combination of agentic and communal communication techniques. Nevertheless, many women strongly resist the notion they need to manage their impressions. They tell us such things as, "That wouldn't be me," "I'd feel like a phony doing that," or "I am who I am, and I am not going to change." But if a woman is serious about advancing in her career, such an attitude is tantamount to saying, "I want to play the competitive promotion game but I am going to tie one hand behind my back."

Andie: A few years ago, I was handling a major tax case in which the principal IRS trial lawyer was a "man's man," an avid sports fan, and a hunter. Quite literally, I could find nothing to talk with him about except the weather and the tax case. But my job was to settle this case on terms that were favorable for my client. If that sort of settlement was going to happen, someone needed to establish rapport with this IRS lawyer, and that was unlikely to be me. So I brought onto our team one of my male partners who was also a sports fan and a man's man. And you know what? The two of them bonded, and the client got a great settlement.

Most of us have probably experienced situations similar to Andie's, when it was helpful to bring another person onto a team because that person had talents or qualities that were needed but missing. Doing this might be called "team impression management"—making sure that your team is able to make the impressions it needs to make to get the job done.

But sometimes, *you* are the whole team, as is the case when the job to be done is advancing *your own* career. When this is the situation, managing "your team's" impressions is solely up to you. If decisiveness is called for, you have to provide it. And when a sense of inclusiveness and warmth is needed, that's up to you, too. This has nothing to do with being inauthentic and everything to do with getting the job done. You wouldn't hesitate to bring another person onto a team if that person's qualities were needed for the job at hand. And, when that job is advancing your own career, you shouldn't hesitate to bring on a new or different communication style if that is what it will take for you to get *that* job done.

But doesn't that require you to be inauthentic, a phony, and not true to yourself? No, no, and no. To effectively manage your impressions you need to be deeply connected with your own feelings. When you are, you are able to draw on the many different aspects and qualities that make you who you are. Managing your impressions is making sure that the impressions you make put the spotlight on *your* most appropriate and effective qualities for that particular situation.[5] Your objective is to present the right aspect of your personality at the right time. This requires high self-monitoring and the use of varied communication techniques. Putting those skills together may not be easy, but it is certainly not being phony.

Another reason women often resist impression management is that they think it will force them to conform to traditional gender stereotypes, and they find this offensive. Managing the impressions you make to advance your career does not require you to accept gender stereotypes, but it does require you to accept reality. Stereotypes about leadership, power, and potential are pervasive facts of life in most career contexts. Therefore, if you are striving for career success, you are playing a competitive game in which these stereotypes provide many of the most important rules.

Andie: At a recent gender communication workshop I told the following story: I was mentoring Ellen, who lived in a different city. I had dealt with her only by phone and e-mail, so when she told me she was being criticized by many of her supervisors as a sloppy thinker, I was puzzled. I had found Ellen to be sharp and focused. So the next

(Continued)

time I was in her city, I went to visit Ellen in person. She was dressed in what I learned was her normal work outfit, which was so casual it was hard for me to tell if she was wearing her pajamas or a sweat suit. Ellen told me she was nervous about an important meeting the next week when she would be interacting with some key company decision makers. I asked her a number of questions about the meeting and why she was nervous. I then stuck my neck out and suggested that she go to a local department store and ask the personal shopper to help her "dress like a banker." Ellen was taken aback by my suggestion and, I think, a little offended. But after we talked for a while, she agreed and attended the meeting dressed in a dark pants suit and low heels.

After the meeting, she reported to me that reactions to her had been entirely different from those she normally experienced. I don't know how much of the change was the result of Ellen's clothing, the increased self-confidence she had because of her new "look," or an alignment of the stars. But what I do know is that Ellen started dressing "like a banker" every day, and I never again heard that she was being criticized as a sloppy thinker.

Ellen's story is interesting in itself, but the most telling thing to come out of that workshop is what I learned afterward. Several women participants criticized my presentation to people who had not been there. These women said that I had advised Ellen to be inauthentic and to buy into traditional stereotypes. After hearing this, I had two distinct reactions. First, I realized I had not done a good job of communicating my message during that workshop. Although I have spent much of my professional life working with women to develop effective ways of overcoming biases resulting from gender stereotypes, I must have come across as insensitive to issues of personal integrity and insufficiently forceful in my condemnation of gender biases. (This was a strong hint that I needed to work on my own impression management.) But my second and more important reaction was one of extraordinary sadness. I realized that the women who had criticized me were unlikely to get as far as they wanted to in their own careers if they really thought that a woman would lose her authenticity if she didn't go to important meetings dressed in her pajamas. We sell ourselves, our abilities, and our potential by the impressions we make. And pajamas were not making the impression Ellen needed to make.

A third reason women often resist consciously managing their impressions is because they assume they don't need to, that if they just do a good job, they will be recognized as highly qualified and, therefore, advanced as they deserve to be. But, the working world seldom operates in this way. Skill, competence, and hard work are certainly necessary, but they are usually not sufficient for career success. Consider the skills we identified at the beginning of this chapter as necessary for career advancement: social presence, organizational intelligence, political savvy, *and* impressive job performance. All of these skills—except job performance—involve impression management. Promotion decisions generally depend on highly subjective judgments about potential or promotability.[6] Therefore, if you are going to move up in your organization, you need to be noticed by your supervisors and colleagues as someone with promotability; someone clearly able to perform at the next level; and someone whose advancement will benefit your company. To be noticed in these ways requires you to manage your impressions. But—and this is the key difference between career advancement for a woman and a man—you need *not* to be noticed as a woman who runs afoul of gender stereotypes. And this also requires careful impression management.

SELF-MONITORING

As we argued earlier in this chapter, your ability to effectively manage your impressions depends on acute self-awareness, that is, high self-monitoring.

Andie: During the summer between my second and third year of law school, I worked at a large law firm, enjoying the variety and challenge of my projects and the mix of people with whom I was working. Throughout the summer, I received high praise from many of the partners, so I was shocked when I did not get an offer to work there after graduation. When I asked why, I was told that a senior partner said I would be offered a job only "over his dead body." When I heard this,

(Continued)

I was deeply troubled. I had met this man only once for, maybe, five minutes and handled only one small project for him. As far as I knew, I had done a good job on the project.

I thought back to our brief meeting. When I was called to his office, his door was open and he was sitting with his feet on his desk and his hands behind his head (one of the high-power posing positions we discuss in chapter 4). I knocked on the doorframe to catch his attention. He looked my way and motioned toward the corner of his office. I was young and eager and had been told always to shake hands when introducing myself. So, I walked toward his desk, extended my hand, and introduced myself. He stood up and shook my hand. I sat down in one of the chairs across from his desk. He gave me the assignment; I thanked him and left his office. I did the assignment and I never gave our five-minute meeting another thought. Not, that is, until I was told I would not work at "his" firm. As I replayed our brief meeting, the reality of the situation finally struck me. I had totally missed the signals he had given me. By walking toward his desk and extending my hand, I unintentionally forced him to take his feet off his desk and stand up. And by sitting down in one of his guest chairs rather than on the low couch in the far corner of his office, I had come across as an assertive, pushy, uppity woman. I had been agentic when a large dose of communal had been called for.

As I have recounted this story over the years, I am often asked whether I would have behaved differently if I had then been a better self-monitor. The answer is "of course." I would have been aware of how uncomfortable I made him by forcing him to stand up. I would have tried to balance my self-confidence with a softer, more deferential style. I probably would not have taken a seat in the corner of his office but I would have been alert to the discomfort and disapproval I was provoking. I might not have been able to change the eventual outcome, but I certainly would have understood what I was actually communicating.

When you are a high self-monitor you read the communication cues other people are giving you and adjust your own communication to make the impression you want to make. You observe the situation to determine "who" you need to be and "how" you need to behave. A low self-monitor is controlled from within by her individual opinions and attitudes, and she is determined to remain "herself" no matter what the situation. It is hardly surprising, therefore, that study after study finds that high self-monitors consistently and decisively beat out low self-monitors for career promotions. High self-monitors advance further, and more often, than low self-monitors, whether they stay at one company or move from company to company.[7]

> *Al:* For many years, I had a partner who was an exceptionally talented lawyer. His practice was primarily mergers and acquisitions that involved lengthy and intense negotiating sessions. His negotiating ability was superb: he could ingratiate himself when this was called for, cajole and prod as needed, and storm out of the room if a threat to crater the deal might win an important concession. Whatever his tactic, however, it was always purposeful and calculated. He was never really angry—or pleased—he was just working to get the job done.
>
> This partner disagreed with several fundamental firm policies, however. And here—where he should have been at his best as a negotiator—he was terrible. He would get angry, sarcastic, and petulant. It got so bad that the other partners didn't want to deal with him. He eventually felt so isolated he left the firm. This brilliant lawyer was a very high self-monitor when it came to negotiating on behalf of a client. But when it came to negotiating on his own behalf, his self-monitoring ability was zero. He simply could not step back from himself, evaluate what he needed to do to achieve his personal objective, and control his communication to the extent needed to do that. It was a very sad situation.

As you move up the career ladder your job responsibilities shift from specific tasks to leadership, motivation, and coordination.[8] To be successful in these higher-level positions, you need to be able to maintain and manage the good opinions of others.[9] Not surprisingly, therefore, successful senior managers in all businesses and professions are high self-monitors.[10]

OBSERVING NONVERBAL COMMUNICATION

In the remainder of this chapter we offer a series of observations about the meaning of specific pieces of other people's nonverbal behavior. Because nonverbal behavior can be difficult to control, it will often be your most important source of information about the impressions you are making on the people with whom you are dealing.

Facial Expressions

Facial expressions will typically provide you with the most important clues about people's reactions to you. While there are many facial expressions, six of them are universal, so you will need to be able to recognize and respond to them.

- If someone is angry, her eyebrows will be lowered, her eyes wide and staring, her forehead wrinkled, and her lips either pressed together firmly or open and teeth clenched.
- If someone is disgusted, the bridge of her nose will be wrinkled, her upper lip raised, and her chin is likely to be jutting up.
- If someone is fearful, her eyes will be open wide, closed, or looking down, her eyebrows will be raised, and her mouth slightly open or with the corners turned down.
- If someone is happy, the corners of her mouth will be raised (with her mouth either open or closed), wrinkles will form at the sides of her eyes, and her eyebrows will be slightly raised.
- If someone is sad, the corners of her mouth will turn down, the inner portion of her eyebrows will raise up, and her eyes will be cast downward and might be damp from tears.
- If someone is surprised, her eyes will open wide so you can see their whites, her eyebrows will be raised, her mouth will be open with her jaw dropped slightly, and her head will be held back or tilted to the side.

The better you know another person, the better you will be at reading her nonverbal behavior. When you do not know a person well, you should be attentive to all aspects of her behavior so that after an encounter you can "read back" into her facial expressions the content you will want to be aware of the next time you interact with her.

Eye Contact

Eye contact is often the surest indication of a positive connection between two people. In the United States and Europe, direct eye contact is generally recognized as showing attentiveness, honesty, confidence, and respect. How someone establishes, maintains, terminates, or resists eye contact tells you a lot about what she is thinking and feeling. Subject to cultural differences, some messages you should be able to pick up from a person's eyes include the following:

- If someone looks directly at you, she is likely to be sincere or confident in what she is saying.
- If someone stares at you for an extended period of time, she is likely to be angry, combative, threatening, or trying to assert dominance.
- If someone looks up toward the ceiling, she might be deep in thought, trying to recall a prepared remark, or just plain bored.
- If someone looks down, she is likely to be embarrassed, ashamed, defensive, submissive, threatened, or feeling guilty. Culture often matters here. If the person is from a country where eye contact is considered to be rude, looking down might actually be a way of showing respect.
- If someone looks off to the side rather than directly at you, she might be feeling guilty, something (or someone) has caught her attention, or she is distracted.
- If someone looks around the room, she is likely to be bored, nervous, or lying.
- If someone won't look you in the eye, she is likely to be uncomfortable, insecure, or submissive. She is unlikely to want to offend you.

- If someone looks up at you with her head down, she may be coy or confused. If she is also frowning, she is likely to be critical of something you have said or done.
- If someone looks at the clock, her watch, or over your shoulder, she may be disinterested, arrogant, or simply looking for someone else.

Smiling

Someone showing friendliness, happiness, or pleasure is likely to smile. But a person smiles for all sorts of other reasons. She might be smiling to hide her discomfort, embarrassment, apprehension, dishonesty, nervousness, suspicion, anger, or misery.[11] You should be able to identify a genuine smile of pleasure, however, because it will light up her face, extend to her eyes, and wrinkle the sides of her eyes. Because most people can flash a social smile on command, you need to keep in mind that a social or phony smile is not likely to extend to the eyes.

Gender stereotypes can influence the ways in which we interpret and react to others' smiles. Because of gender stereotypes, people expect women to smile more than men, and women are likely to accept the validity of the stereotype. Therefore, just because a woman is smiling does not mean she likes you or agrees with what you are saying. She might be trying to appear likable and pleasant, or she might feel awkward or uncomfortable, be interested in restoring harmony, or be seeking to appease a more powerful person. It is much harder to read a woman's smiles than to read a man's smiles. You have to pay attention to all of her behavior, what her eyes and facial muscles reveal, and the appropriateness of the smile in the particular context.

Head Nodding

Women frequently nod their heads to show attentiveness, not necessarily to indicate agreement, as it almost always does in men. Men typically don't nod their heads unless they agree with what is being said. If a man does not nod his head while you are speaking, don't get flustered or ask him if he understood your points. Continue with confidence and wait for his reaction.

KEY TAKEAWAYS

■ Learn what type of self-monitor you are. Answer the questions on the Self-Monitoring Scale at http://personality-testing.info/tests/SMS.

■ Improve your level of self-monitoring. You don't need to psycho-analyze yourself, but you do need to have sufficiently robust conversations with yourself to be able to describe (to yourself) exactly how you feel at any given time. Study how other people react to you in different contexts. If their reactions are not the ones you would like, try a different communication style.

■ Packaging of your message is vital. The objective of impression management is to ensure that your ideas are received warmly and treated fairly. This will not happen if you are focused solely on the content of your message. Its packaging is equally important. And, that packaging will control the impression you make.

■ Never, ever, believe it is your fault when you encounter gender bias.

4

Your Attitudes Matter

As you seek career advancement you should have two basic objectives: first, to be noticed as someone who is competent, confident, and capable of handling tasks and situations expected of positions senior to the one you now hold. Your second objective is to prevent your competence, confidence, and capability from being seen as characteristic of a pushy, unpleasant, and socially insensitive woman who is violating traditional gender stereotypes. There is an obvious tension in these objectives, for it is hard to get yourself noticed as a leader without also being noticed as a woman who is not conforming to gender stereotypes. This tension is one of the primary reasons achieving a full measure of career success is so problematic for so many women. As we have just discussed, your commitment to impression management and high self-monitoring is fundamentally important if you are to deal with this tension effectively. But so are the two other pieces of attuned gender communication: (1) the cultivation and display of positive psychological and mental attitudes, and (2) the knowledge and ability to use the communication techniques that can help you shape and change the impressions you make. We will start to discuss the essential communication techniques in the next chapter. In this chapter, our concern is with the key attitudes for career success—grit, a positive perspective on your abilities, a coping sense of humor, and a confident self-image—and how you can develop and strengthen these attitudes.

GRIT

Grit involves perseverance, self-discipline, tenacity, persistence, and fortitude. It is the ability to sustain effort toward a long-term objective despite failure, adversity, and plateaus on your journey, the capacity to pursue a goal without giving up because of setbacks. Malcolm Gladwell, in his book *Outliers*, writes that grit is one of the few personality traits that is shared by prominent leaders in all fields.[1] A person with grit takes the long view: she plans, executes, and reformulates her plans until she has one that works. Because of the gender stereotypes operating in your workplace, frustrations and setbacks are highly likely. You will need grit to keep you going.

Andie: Anne is a very close friend of mine. Many years ago, after spending six years as a public interest attorney, she decided to pursue a new career in the private practice of law. While Anne recognized the importance of the work she was doing, she realized she was not growing because she was not being intellectually challenged. She was interested in the complexity of the legal work involved in employee pension and benefits planning. So she sent her résumé to every law firm in her city with a significant employee benefits practice. Anne had stellar credentials, but she did not receive a single positive response.

She came to me to discuss her career dilemma. Together we developed a plan to improve her employment prospects. Anne would read everything she could find about employee benefits law. She would attend conferences on current legal developments in the area, and she would take all the continuing legal education programs available. She did this full time for about six months. Anne prepared a new résumé that showcased her extensive knowledge and the seriousness of her commitment.

With her résumé in hand, Anne got an appointment at one of the premier law firms in Chicago. She offered to start as a first-year lawyer (without credit or compensation for her six years out of law school

(Continued)

or her substantial expertise). The law firm hired her, and over time she distinguished herself as one of the most accomplished and prominent benefits lawyers in the country. A few years ago she was lured away from the law firm by a large multinational corporation, where she now supervises employee benefits for its many thousands of employees. Anne has grit.

The sort of women we think about when we discuss grit are Marie Sklodowska Curie, Joanne (J. K.) Rowling, Misty Copeland, and the first two women to become U.S. Army Rangers. When Curie was denied a university education in Poland because she was a woman, she pursued her studies in secret while working as a tutor and governess to finance her and her sister's educations. She moved to Paris, studied at the University of Paris, and lived a subsistence existence in an unheated garret. She began to work with her future husband in a cramped, poorly equipped laboratory. Before being awarded a PhD, Curie published more than thirty-two scientific papers and she and her husband were awarded the Nobel Prize in physics. Less than ten years later, she alone was awarded the Nobel Prize in chemistry. Despite encountering gender discrimination and xenophobia, Curie pursued her goals fearlessly. She had grit.

During her 2008 commencement address at Harvard University, Rowling discussed how she began to write her first novel when she was recently divorced, had a small child, was unemployed, and lived in such poverty she was receiving government assistance. She refused to let these conditions define her. Rather than becoming discouraged, Rowling directed all of her energy into accomplishing the central goal of her life: finishing her novel about a school for wizards.[2] Four years later, *Harry Potter and the Sorcerer's Stone* was published and the rest is history. Rowling has grit.

Copeland, who in 2015 became a principal ballerina at American Ballet Theatre, is an unlikely dancer. She did not start training until she was thirteen, and then only with free classes at the local Boys & Girls Club. At that time, she was living in a motel room with her mother and five siblings. Copeland is an athletic African American whose body does not conform to the image of what a classical ballerina's should be. Nevertheless, a ballerina is what she wanted to be and a ballerina she became. Now in her early thirties, Copeland is the first star ballerina to also become a celebrity, advertising powerhouse, and the subject of a major documentary.[3] Copeland has grit.

In August of 2015, Capt. Kristen Griest and 1st Lt. Shaye Haver became the first female graduates of the grueling Army Ranger's training program. Ranger training requires physical strength and speed, but it also requires the passion and stamina to stick with long-term goals. Griest and Haver met exactly the same standards as the ninety-four men with whom they graduated: hand-to-hand combat, swimming with heavy gear, carrying fallen comrades, and dropping from helicopters. The opportunity to train with the men allowed them to push themselves and expand their capabilities.[4] It is hard to think of anyone with more grit than Griest and Haver.

Not surprisingly, grit is the most important noncognitive predictor of success for women at the U.S.'s two hundred largest law firms. In a 2005 study, researchers found that the women with grit navigated their workplace challenges (negative feedback from senior lawyers, self-doubts, and the sometimes overwhelming pace and volume of the work itself) far better than women without grit.[5] These women who succeeded in the world of big law believed that if they stuck with their goals despite frustrations and failures, they would reach those goals—and they were correct. Their success is underscored by a 2012 report by McKinsey & Company, which found that resilience—the ability to persevere in the face of challenges and setbacks—is a trait common to successful women no matter what their career path.[6]

But if grit is important, even essential, for career success, how do you get it? Not everyone starts out as gritty as Curie and Copeland. You can strengthen your grit, however, in a number of ways. For instance, set a clear, long-term goal for yourself and keep track of how you perform in relation to it. Have you made plans to guide you? Are you revising your plans as necessary? Are you zealously following up on what you need to do next to get to your goal? When you don't perform up to your own—or your supervisor's—satisfaction, are you studying why? What sorts of things discourage you? Motivate you? This exercise is meant to force you to be attentive to the behavior patterns that will allow you to move steadily toward your career objective.

In this regard, you may find the Grit Project, an initiative of the American Bar Association's Commission on Women, to be a valuable resource. The Grit Project offers advice and insight to help women pursue their goals despite failures, frustrations, and setbacks.[7] Although the Grit Project was created to assist attorneys, its exercises and advice are valuable no matter your career path.

Another approach to developing your grit is to step back and consider the challenges you face from another person's perspective. Think about how a person whose grit you admire would address the problem or difficulty you are facing. Attempting to emulate the actions and thoughts of a particularly gritty person can be a strong motivator. If you have never known anyone like that, read more about Curie, Rowling, Copeland, Griest, and Haver, or another contemporary or historical figure whose persistence and tenacity you particularly admire. Grit is all about not giving up on yourself and your career. If you really want to succeed, don't give up on developing grit.

POSITIVE PERSPECTIVE

Grit is persistence in the pursuit of a goal despite adversity. That sort of sustained effort is difficult unless you believe that your persistence will eventually pay off. To maintain that belief you need a positive perspective on your own abilities and capabilities, a perspective that you will get better—smarter, more sensible, and more skilled—through hard work, challenges, difficulty, failure, and achievement. Psychologists refer to this sort of perspective as a growth mindset.[8] When you have a growth mindset you think about your intelligence, skills, and common sense not as fixed and static but as assets that can be developed and improved. You view mistakes as learning opportunities and frustrations as growing pains. Such a positive perspective allows you to remain focused on your career objectives because you are learning from your setbacks and growing stronger as a result of your failures. With this sort of attitude, the barriers to your advancement created by gender bias can take on a more positive aspect: challenges are not roadblocks but opportunities for growth.

The trick, of course, is to be able to assess in every circumstance what you need to do to improve and what changes you must make in your behavior for that to happen. There are remarkable people who do this on their own, but most of us need help, criticism, evaluation, and advice from others. Having your performance critiqued is rarely easy. When you have a positive perspective on your abilities, however, you are likely to have the courage to reveal your weaknesses, the confidence not to become defensive in the face of negative judgments, and the willingness to undertake needed changes.

Atul Gawande is a highly accomplished surgeon, as well as a staff writer for the *New Yorker* and a best-selling author. He had been a surgeon for eight years when he realized that his skills had not significantly improved since his third year of practice. He didn't know if he was at the top of his game or just stuck in a rut. So he invited a retired surgeon he greatly admired to observe and critique his performance during a surgery of a type he had performed many times. The other surgeon watched and took notes, a lot of notes: he observed Gawande's elbows were too high, his use of a magnifying loupe restricted his peripheral vision, he was not paying attention to things he should, and much more. When he got the report, Gawande was taken aback by how many things he was doing wrong, but he also realized the other surgeon was right. He had been unable to evaluate his own performance and would never have known how to become a better surgeon without outside help. By deliberately seeking a rigorous evaluation of his performance, Gawande acknowledged that he probably had shortcomings, and (more importantly) that he could overcome them and improve. This sort of behavior is the hallmark of a person with a positive perspective on his abilities.

In your career, you probably don't need to invite someone to critique your performance. In all likelihood, you are receiving regular evaluations in the form of performance reviews, criticisms of specific projects, and feedback from colleagues and supervisors. If you are not getting this sort of objective, detailed evaluation, you need to seek it out. But one way or the other, you need to recognize that outside, objective criticism is the most important resource you have for improvement. With a positive perspective on your abilities, you will treasure the (fair) criticism you receive.

HUMOR

A healthy sense of humor is as valuable in your professional life as it is in your personal life. Physiologically, when you laugh or smile, endorphins are released into your bloodstream, reducing stress, increasing your sense of happiness, and improving your ability to cope with difficult situations. Humor can also improve your ability to connect with and influence other people. A person with a cheerful, friendly, good-natured sense of humor is generally seen by others as happy, well-adjusted, and creative. More important for your career, a person with a sense of humor is typically seen as approachable, likable, and trustworthy.

Gender stereotypes foster discrimination, but they also make many career situations extremely stressful. A strong coping sense of humor is a great ally in dealing with this sort of stress. When you have the ability to inject humor into a stressful situation, you become more self-confident and less hesitant to expose yourself to potentially difficult interactions, performances, and projects supervised by jerks.

Andie: I was once called into a meeting that was already in progress. Just as I walked into the room, our client (who had his back to the door) said, "Andie, is that a girl? I can't work with a girl." I put my hand on his shoulder and said something like, "I think we should start our introduction over again. Don't you?" So I walked out of the room, came back in, shook hands with the client, and proceeded as though nothing had happened. Over the years I worked with him on several

(Continued)

projects, and occasionally we laughed together about our first meeting. When I look back, I often wonder what would have happened if my first reaction had been to take offense or get angry, rather than to smile, make a joke, and move on.

When you can achieve a degree of emotional distance between yourself and the frustrating situations you encounter in your workplace, you will find it much easier to use humor in those situations. By putting a distance between yourself and your difficult interactions, you will find that these interactions increasingly take on a humorous aspect. You don't have to laugh out loud or tell a joke, but an amused "Can you believe it?" or even a wry grin can be incredibly beneficial in helping you and the people with whom you are working cope with highly stressful situations.

Al: Laura had just received a major promotion and was now in charge of her company's nationwide transportation facilities. As she traveled from one facility to another introducing herself and getting to know her direct reports, everything seemed to be going well. That is, until Laura got to the largest of the facilities. She was introduced to the employees—almost all of whom were men—by a man she later learned was a close friend of Joe, the man whose job she had taken. Laura listened in horror as Joe's friend finished his introduction by saying he didn't think Laura would be "able to carry Joe's jockstrap." As she took the microphone, the employees were all laughing. After a moment of panic, Laura smiled and said, "Well, I think that's a very good thing because I certainly wouldn't want to carry Joe's jockstrap." This time there was even more laughter, and Laura proceeded with her brief remarks before a respectful group of employees. Without her humorous comeback, Laura believes she would have faced a long and difficult time trying to establish her leadership. Because of her quip, however, she established herself as someone who could take a joke, but also as someone who could hold her own in the face of a hostile male audience.

To understand a bit more about the benefits of a coping sense of humor, let's look at the common and powerful stereotype that women are not good at math. A recent study sought to determine whether a strong coping sense of humor would allow women to do mathematics without being negatively affected by this stereotype. The researchers had a group of undergraduate women complete the Coping Humor Scale before taking a math test. Half of the women were given the math test under conditions that made the math stereotype prominent, and the other half were given the math test under conditions unaffected by the math stereotype. In the conditions of stereotype threat, women who had a strong coping sense of humor scored higher than other women. In the conditions without stereotype threat, a sense of humor makes no difference in the women's performance. The clear conclusion, according to the researchers, is that a coping sense of humor helps women minimize or overcome the effects of stereotype threat.[9]

In another study, humor was found to provide a powerful tool for managing anxiety. Study participants were told that they would receive an electric shock.[10] In advance of the anticipated shock, some participants listened to a humorous audiotape, while others listened to a non-humorous audiotape. Those participants who listened to the humorous tape were found to have experienced less anxiety waiting for the electric shock than those who listened to a non-humorous recording.[11]

Andie: I was waiting to be interviewed on a live television news program about a legal topic, leveraged buyouts, that was then of current interest. I had been told the topic a week before and was well prepared. The plan was for the interviewer to go over his questions with me for about five minutes before we went live. When I arrived at the studio, the scene was hectic and fast moving. After watching part of the interview immediately before mine, I shook hands with the interviewer and we sat down in front of the cameras. The interviewer then said, "We're going to talk about mutual funds." "No," I said, "I was invited to speak about leveraged buyouts." He said, "I don't want to talk about that." The producer yelled, "THREE." I asked if we had three minutes, and I was told, "No. Three seconds."

(Continued)

As a child, I had a recurrent dream about getting to school, taking off my winter coat, and finding I forgot to put on my Brownie uniform that morning. When I learned I had three seconds before a live television interview about a topic I was totally unprepared to discuss, my first thought was, "Did I put my clothes on this morning?" I looked down and was so relieved to see I was dressed that I smiled as I looked up. That was the first camera shot of me: smiling and looking comfortable. I must admit that I have no recollection of the rest of that interview, but friends said I did great. I now purposely use that technique whenever I am in a public situation and start to feel nervous; I remind myself that at least I have my clothes on, I smile, and I proceed forward.

Approaching challenging situations with emotional distance and a humorous perspective allows you to see these situations as occasions for innovation and adaptation, and not apprehension and anxiety. Humor helps you get the job done. Jokes and laughter are not necessary, but a wry perspective on yourself and what is happening around you often is.

SELF-IMAGE

Real career success depends on many things, one of which is an ability to project a self-image that is confident, powerful, creative, and in control. When you are anxious, worried about your ability to perform up to your potential, or concerned you will be seen as less competent than you are, you may find it particularly difficult to project this sort of self-image. In these sorts of stressful situations, it is enormously helpful to have techniques available that will boost your positive sense of your self. You can't just tell yourself to project self-confidence. That is likely to be no more effective than telling yourself not to be stressed when you are experiencing great stress.

Fortunately, there are two proven techniques that will—at least for a relatively short period of time—increase your personal, psychological sense of yourself as strong, confident, and capable: mind priming and power posing.

Mind Priming

Our minds are "primed"—that is, conditioned, programmed, prepared, and trained—in all sorts of ways. The stereotypes with which you operate prime you to think about particular people in particular ways. When you are exposed to rude or cooperative behavior, your mind is primed to behave more rudely or cooperatively than you would otherwise.[12] And when you are told that women are not good at math, you are being primed to doubt women's ability to do mathematics. In all of these instances, your mind is being conditioned or programmed without your conscious involvement in the process. But you can also consciously prime your own mind, to adopt, for example, attitudes and outlooks that are valuable for your career advancement. This sort of conscious mind priming can also be called altering your mindset, changing your frame of mind, or purposely triggering particular psychological associations. But whatever you call it, conscious mind priming works.

One way to prime your own mind is to take a short period of time to think in a focused way—best done by writing—about an occasion when you felt particularly powerful, a time of great happiness, or the achievements you have already made. By taking five minutes to do this before a high-stakes interview, negotiation, evaluation, speech, presentation, or group meeting, you will perform in a more confident, commanding, and self-assured manner;[13] display more powerful nonverbal behavior;[14] and increase your sense of confidence, optimism, and control.[15] Priming your mind in this way will also reduce your own anxiety and stress, and, therefore, increase the sense others have of you as a confident leader.[16]

We find that many of the women we coach are highly skeptical about conscious mind priming. Even when we tell them about a 2012 study in which participants who had primed their minds by writing about a time they felt particularly powerful were far more successful in negotiating mock business deals than those that didn't,[17] they are still inclined to say it wouldn't work for them. Nevertheless, when we are able to convince a woman to try the technique, she inevitably becomes a committed mind primer.

Andie: I am continually recommending that a woman prime herself for power shortly before undertaking a new or particularly stressful activity. The following comments are typical of those I have gotten back from women who have used the technique:

- "I primed before my interview by spending five minutes concentrating, really concentrating, on a time I felt especially powerful. I got the promotion and job transfer I dreamed of. My boss told me that the interviewer said I was the most confident and qualified applicant for promotion."
- "Before a recent interview I spent fifteen minutes drafting a summary of my qualifications for the position and reflecting on my prior career achievements. During the interview I noticed that I was neither nervous nor anxious; I was poised and focused. My rapport with the interviewer felt natural and our conversation flowed freely. I have never walked out of an interview feeling more upbeat or more positive. And, I got the job."
- "I am usually very nervous going into what I know will be a difficult negotiation. This time, I took your advice and spent five minutes writing down my strengths as a negotiator and why the changes I wanted to make in the contract made sense and were fully justified. I never became nervous or lost my self-confidence. The outcome was exactly what I had hoped for. Thank you so much. It totally works."

Positive mind priming works because the way you "talk" to yourself affects the way you see yourself; the way you see yourself affects the way you act; and the way you act affects the impressions others form of you. The behavioral changes initially triggered by mind priming are generally short-lived (from a few minutes to an hour), but this sort of intentional self-conditioning can have long-lasting effects. In a study of three-person groups, for example, the one person in each group who had mind primed herself was seen as the group leader at a rate nearly twice that expected by chance.[18] And, the person initially perceived to be the group leader is generally given more information and more opportunities to speak than others. Consequently, she has the opportunity to perform at a higher level, which reinforces her leadership position. In other words, the "I am strong, I am a leader" mindset for which you prime yourself for a group meeting can have a lasting effect on your status and influence within that group.

Power Posing

Mind priming is about thinking your way—in a quite specific manner—to more confident and powerful behavior. In other words, you can have conversations with yourself that decisively affect the way you feel about yourself. You can also affect the way you feel about yourself by adjusting not your mind but your body. By assuming and holding certain poses for a short period of time, say two minutes, you can significantly boost your self-confidence, sense of strength, risk and pain tolerance, and the forcefulness of your physical presence.

The use of body posture to increase self-confidence is often referred to as power posing, and its effect is strikingly illustrated by a recent study. Participants were told to imagine they were about to be interviewed for their dream job. For two minutes, half of the participants assumed a pose identified with high power—think Wonder Woman with her legs apart and her hands on her hips—while the other half assumed a pose associated with low power—think sitting with shoulders slumped, arms close to the body, and legs together. The participants were then given five minutes to prepare a presentation. After the preparation, each participant made a five-minute speech about her or his qualifications and why she or he should be hired. No correlation was found between the poses the participants assumed and the quality of the content of their speeches. Nevertheless, the participants who had assumed higher-power poses prior to their interviews were consistently rated as more powerful, more confident, and more dominant than the other participants. Moreover, the high-power posers were consistently judged to have maintained better composure, projected more confidence, and presented more enthusiastic speeches than did the low-power posers.[19]

This is such a dramatic result that it is worth focusing carefully on the poses associated with high power and low power. There are good pictures of these poses in Amy Cuddy's 2012 TED Talk—a video well worth watching.[20] High-power poses include the Wonder Woman pose, the "totally confident pose" (sitting with your feet on your desk, hands behind your head, and elbows spread wide); the "all business pose" (standing and leaning forward with your hands resting on a table and your shoulders square, your chin up, and your eyes straight ahead); and the "victory stance" (standing tall with your legs apart, your head raised, and your arms held in a V high above your head). Any of these poses, held for at least two minutes before a high-stakes situation, can help you feel more powerful. And feeling more powerful also means you are feeling less anxious, inhibited, or fearful, attitudes that get in the way of your performing at the top of your game.

Poses associated with low power all involve non-expansive, shrinking postures: sitting hunched or slouched down in your chair, hanging your head low, stooping your shoulders, or standing with your body stooped. Low-power poses can hurt your confidence and sense of presence in high-stakes situations.

Al: I recently met with Jasmine, who was trying to transition back into a career. She had had several disappointing interviews that did not lead to job offers. I suggested that before her next interview she try power posing. Jasmine was dubious but agreed to give it a try. She reported that the whole dynamic of the interview process changed for her. She felt more confident, and the interviewer seemed to pick up on this. Instead of the scheduled thirty minutes, her interview lasted close to an hour, and before she left Jasmine was introduced to several other decision makers, and a follow-up interview was scheduled.

One particularly interesting study looked at the effect of power posing on risk taking. Half of the participants assumed high-power poses and half assumed low-power poses. All participants were then given $2 and told they could roll dice at even odds either to win $4 or to lose the initial $2. Eighty-six percent of the high-power posers rolled the dice, as opposed to only 60 percent of the low-power posers.[21]

In another study, power posing for two minutes was shown to increase testosterone, a hormone linked to confidence and assertiveness, by 20 percent and to decrease cortisol, a hormone linked to stress, by 25 percent.[22] This combination of hormones increases your sense of control, engagement, and capacity. With high testosterone, you behave in a more assertive way; you don't hang back, aren't diffident, and don't hide your contributions. With low cortisol, you experience less stress and feel less pressure.

Like so much else in social sciences research, the concept that posture is power is hardly surprising. Think about nonhuman primates. You know immediately which great ape is the alpha male in the family by the way he carries himself—and other apes don't. Open body postures with confident, bold gestures indicate high power, while constricted, closed-in postures indicate low power. By playing the great ape (in private) before high-stakes professional interactions, you can significantly increase both your confidence and sense of power.

Andie: Some women were following the principles of power posing long before it had a name. Barb is a friend and a very successful senior manager. She is a tiny woman, and finds she can be ignored in mixed-gender meetings. When Barb wants to make an important point, she gets up to get a cup of coffee or a glass of water. Then, while she is standing with the drink in one hand, she puts her other hand on the top of her chair and starts talking. Standing in this pose, she is never ignored and her comments are always given careful consideration. Getting a drink is her excuse for standing up, but once on her feet she will stay up until she has effectively made her points.

KEY TAKEAWAYS

■ Determine the extent of your grit by taking the grit test at http://www.sas.upenn.edu/~duckwort/images/17-item%20Grit%20and%20Ambition.040709.pdf.

■ If you want to be grittier, follow Eleanor Roosevelt's advice to "do the thing you think you cannot do." This means stretching yourself and picking yourself up after failures.

■ The belief in the possibility of growth makes it easier to stick with difficult, long-term projects. Believe in your own ability to get better—smarter, more sensible, and more task proficient.

■ Develop a positive perspective and a growth mindset. Take the mindset test at http://mindsetonline.com/testyourmindset/step1.php. Seek out challenging assignments that involve activities completely new to you, and push yourself.

■ Look at the training tools for the Grit Project to learn more about developing grit and a growth mindset: http://www.americanbar.org/groups/women/initiatives_awards/grit.html. You don't need to be a lawyer to use them.

■ Use humor to deal with tough situations. Test your coping sense of humor at http://academic.csuohio.edu/neuendorf_ka/chs.pdf. If it is low, before going into your next stressful situation, read something humorous, listen to some comedy routines, or watch a funny movie or short video on the Internet.

■ Prime your mind to increase your self-confidence before high-stakes situations. Write a few paragraphs about a time you felt particularly powerful or happy.

■ Strike a pose. Power posing should become part of your behavior before every high-stakes situation. Even if it feels a little weird, it works. And be sure to watch Cuddy's TED Talk on power posing at http://www.ted.com/talks/amy_cuddy_your_body_language_shapes_who_you_are.

PART III

Conversations with Others

5

Nonverbal Behavior

In chapter 3, "Managing the Impressions You Make," we discussed the importance of reading other people's nonverbal behavior in reaction or response to the impressions you are making. These impressions are the result, in large part, of *your* nonverbal behavior, that is, your facial expressions, gestures, voice tone and pitch, nonsubstantive words and phrases, posture, displayed feelings and attitudes, movements, and actions. Through this nonverbal behavior, you communicate a great deal of information about your abilities, accomplishments, self-confidence, and potential. Your ability to manage your impressions, therefore, depends to a significant extent on your ability to manage your nonverbal behavior.

NONVERBAL BEHAVIOR AND STEREOTYPES

Let's look again at common gender stereotypes and catalog some of the sorts of nonverbal behavior associated with them. Women are communal, and communal people are pleasant and approachable; they speak in a soft, often high-pitched voice, hesitate while speaking, use incomplete sentences, maintain a closed body posture with hands held close to the sides, take up little physical space, and rarely maintain direct eye contact; they generally cast their eyes down, lean forward when listening, nod to indicate attentiveness, often touch their face, hair, or jewelry, smile frequently, interrupt others seldom, infrequently seek personal recognition, hold their mouths open slightly, and tilt their heads to the side and up.

By contrast, the common stereotype about men is that they are agentic, and agentic people have power and authority; they speak in a low, firm tone of voice with few hesitations or pitch variations, use full sentences, frequently interrupt others, maintain an open body posture with arms apart, gesture in a calm and controlled but expansive manner, make minimal leg and foot movements, maintain moderately high eye contact, hold a relatively neutral facial expression with the head still, lean back when listening, and nod only to express agreement.

As long as a woman's nonverbal behavior conforms (for the most part) to the communal characteristics, she will be viewed as warm, friendly, and socially sensitive but lacking in ambition and leadership ability. If, however, her nonverbal behavior takes on significant agentic characteristics, her colleagues may become confused, distrustful, and critical. This adverse reaction to agentic women is well illustrated by a 1995 study in which men were found to think that women who exhibited a "high-task style" were less likable, more threatening, and less influential than men exhibiting exactly the same style and delivering exactly the same message. (A high-task style involves nonverbal behavior associated with authority and competence: a rapid rate of speech with a firm tone and few hesitations, an upright posture, a moderately high amount of eye contact, relatively neutral facial expressions, and unobtrusive hand gestures.)[1]

Thus we have another Goldilocks Dilemma: appearing too tough or too soft but rarely just right. Unless you use nonverbal behavior that has strong associations with power and competence, you will never be seen as a leader. But when you exhibit this sort of agentic behavior, you risk being seen as cold, aggressive, and insensitive.[2] Certain of the attitudes we discussed in the preceding chapter—grit, positive perspective, and a confident self-image—lead you to display highly agentic nonverbal behavior because you exhibit power and confidence. The danger, therefore, is that these attitudes can backfire unless you can pair them with communal behavior that projects warmth, inclusiveness, and social sensitivity. This means that your ability to advance in a gender-biased environment depends on your ability to display *at the same time* agentic and communal nonverbal behavior.

In what follows, we look first at expressions, gestures, and postures that can undercut your efforts to be seen as powerful, competent, self-confident, *and* likable; we call this nonverbal behavior "negative behavior." We then discuss nonverbal behavior that will help you project the impressions you want, and we call this "positive behavior."

NEGATIVE NONVERBAL BEHAVIOR

Your nonverbal behavior is negative when the likely reactions to it detract from the impression you want to be making, which will generally be that you are competent, confident, and capable of leadership. Of course, no single piece of nonverbal behavior is ever exhibited in isolation and you will always be judged on your total gestalt. Nevertheless, you want to avoid the possibility that other people will take one aspect of your behavior and use it to interpret the whole of it. Therefore, you should carefully avoid the following sorts of nonverbal behavior.

Appearing Weak

Obviously, the last thing you want is to be seen as a woman with low power, little self-confidence, and poor task competence. We refer to nonverbal behavior often associated with these characteristics as weak. Nonverbal behavior that is typically interpreted as being characteristic of a weak person includes use of a soft, hard-to-hear tone of voice, frequent repetitions and false starts, tentative pauses in a presentation, and the use of frequent filler words such as "hum," "perhaps," "uh-huh," or "don't you think." Weakness is also inferred from a slumped body posture, nervous hand gestures, and averted eyes. You can also come across as weak if you play with your papers or notes, grip your notes tightly with both hands, rub your hands together, hold your papers or laptop in front of your body, cross your arms tightly across your chest with your shoulders slumped and head bowed, close your hands into fists, and frequently giggle, laugh, or touch your hair, jewelry, or clothes.

Andie: Charlotte told me that until she saw a videotape of herself giving a speech, she had no idea she gripped her notes so tightly, hugged them to her chest, or held onto the podium as if it were a life preserver and she were drowning. She realized immediately that her nonverbal behavior was undermining her effort to be seen as a leader within her organization. She realized she was coming across as nervous, scared, and unsure of herself. She asked me to coach her as she practiced speaking. It didn't take very long for Charlotte to get rid of her undesirable nonverbal behavior. She was also able to develop a more confident, powerful behavior. She now looks—and feels—very comfortable speaking before a group.

Many other aspects of nonverbal behavior suggest tentativeness, nervousness, stress, anxiety, or a lack of confidence. These include biting or picking at your nails; twisting, pushing back, tossing, flipping, or adjusting your hair; playing with your watch or a button; wringing your hands; jerky, shaky, and trembling arm movements; and closing your body in by shrinking into a small space and slumping your shoulders. You should try to avoid all of this conduct.

Take videos of yourself and see how you communicate. Assess your nonverbal behavior for indications of weakness; identify your tics, habits, gestures, postures, and expressions that could be sending negative messages about you and your abilities. Then start working to get this sort of behavior out of your communication repertoire.

At the beginning of this discussion of negative nonverbal behavior, we wrote that the impression you "generally" want to make is one of competence, confidence, and leadership ability. But there are times when the impression you want to make is not one of forcefulness but approachability, not ambition but inclusiveness, not assertiveness but friendship. In other words, you do not want to be agentic all the time.

As we have been arguing, your effective management of the impressions you make depends on your ability to use both agentic and communal communication techniques to navigate your way around and through the multiple double binds that gender stereotypes create for women. And communicating in such a way that your positive communal qualities are on full display often depends on you using behavior that we have been characterizing as "weak." So keep in mind that while you do not want to appear weak in situations that call for forceful leadership, you will often need to soften your impressions to avoid a backlash, and this is often best accomplished by the nonverbal behavior that projects warmth and social sensitivity.[3]

Appearing Dominant

Domineering nonverbal behavior is the opposite of weak behavior, but that doesn't mean it is positive. A domineering style involves an open body posture; aggressive gestures, such as pointing your finger directly at another person; speaking in a loud, angry voice; maintaining constant and challenging eye contact; having a stern facial expression; making abrupt movements or gestures; and maintaining an indirect body orientation. A dominant style won't convey competence or likability; it makes you seem ill tempered, even out of control. Women seldom use a domineering style, but be on the alert for any tendencies you might have in this direction and check them.

Appearing Untrustworthy

Your persuasiveness, influence, and likability all depend on other people trusting you. If your nonverbal behavior leads other people to doubt your trustworthiness, it will be difficult for you to make impressions of the sort you want. People are likely to find your behavior suspicious or disturbing if you turn your body away from them while you are addressing them, talk or fidget during meetings or negotiations, or look around the room instead of at the people with whom you are interacting. Significantly, this is the sort of behavior you are likely to exhibit if you are anxious or unsure of yourself, another reason that a confident self-image is so important. When you lack confidence in what you are saying or doing, you can be viewed not just as tentative and uncertain but also as untrustworthy.

POSITIVE NONVERBAL BEHAVIOR

As we have emphasized several times, the successful path through the many Too Hot/Too Cold/Rarely Just Right Dilemmas women face involve presenting yourself as competent *and* likable, powerful *and* warm, forceful *and* inclusive. Nonverbal behavior that can accomplish these dual objectives include the following:

- Your voice: moderate volume, no extreme changes in tone or pitch, and few pauses and hesitations.
- Your body language: relaxed and open body posture with calm, inclusive hand gestures that are smooth, natural, and not exaggerated, leaning slightly forward to listen, and not fidgeting.
- Your eyes: moderate eye contact, not looking down or wandering. In a group, making eye contact with each person.
- Your head: held with chin slightly up.
- Your facial expression: warm and pleasant with frequent smiles and obvious attention.
- Your "mirroring": lean forward if the other person leans forward; lean back if the other person leans back; speak at the same rate and pitch of the other person.

SPECIFIC SITUATIONS AND INTERACTIONS

By looking closely at a variety of specific sorts of nonverbal behavior, we can get a better sense of how you can project your competence and social sensitivity.

Using Space

Power, status, and confidence are all associated with the use of physical space, and the highest-status men tend to take up the most space. Women tend to take up less space than do men, and women generally are quicker than men to retreat from their space to make room for others. Imagine a group of people sitting around a conference table. Before anything is said, our guess is that you can identify the important people by the way they sit, their position at the table, and the amount of space they take up. These are all nonverbal signals of importance.

Your ability to make an impression as a person of confidence and importance will be enhanced if you develop the habit of claiming space: take up as much space as the men do—spread out your papers—and if you only have a few papers, be sure to bring more next time. Spreading out does not mean being sloppy, lounging across several chairs, stretching your arms out to the sides, or pushing other people away. It does mean behaving expansively, maintaining an open body position, resting your arms on the table, and not letting anyone take space away from you. Find a comfortable place to rest your hands. If you are standing, rest them on the podium or the top of a chair, or you can hold them calmly but not too tightly at your side.

Andie: As a young lawyer, I would bring into meetings every book and piece of paper I thought I might need. I rarely (if ever) referred to them, but they provided me with two things: confidence I had them if I needed them and an excuse to take up space. I would get to meetings early so I could sit where I wanted and spread out. Even as a young lawyer I never had a problem getting recognized or listened to at a meeting—and I was never told I was taking up too much space.

You should also take up space by using expansive outward arm gestures. Women tend to gesture toward their bodies; men tend to gesture away from their bodies. This makes women seem smaller while men appear to expand in size. Develop comfortable, smooth gestures that move away from your body. When you are standing, keep your arms away from your body, stand tall, and keep your legs comfortably apart. Space is your friend; use a lot of it.

Just because you are claiming space—displaying power, confidence, and status—does not mean you should be stern or unsmiling. You almost always want to project social sensitivity. This means smiling, having a pleasant facial expression, inviting responses to your comments, and actively expressing agreement with other people's ideas—when you agree and it is appropriate. Space is power, but as a woman, you need to use it with warmth and a sense of inclusiveness.

Handshakes

Your handshake says a great deal about you. Advising women about the all-important handshake seems to be old hat, but we still find too many women getting it wrong. Your handshake needs to be firm, neither vise-like nor wimpy, a confident grasping of the other person's whole hand as you look her in the eyes. You are striving to create an immediate impression of credibility, confidence, and power.

Forget what you might have been told about women and handshakes. If you are seated when someone enters the room and it is time for a handshake, stand up. You are a businesswoman, not a debutante. If you are sitting behind your desk when you are expected to shake someone's hand, step around your desk so that there is nothing awkward or uncomfortable about your body posture. If you are meeting several people at once, stand so that you face each one squarely as you shake his hand. And, if someone—woman or man—extends you a limp hand to shake, do your best to grasp the whole hand and shake it firmly.

Some older men only shake hands with a woman who extends her hand first. This is yet another reason to always be the first to extend your hand. Don't ever be confused or embarrassed when the occasion arises to shake hands: immediately extend your hand to everyone, look each person in the eye, and smile.

Andie: In a recent workshop, I mentioned that an older man might not shake hands with a woman unless she first extends her hand to him. Several of the women immediately started to laugh with relief. They had all been in groups where the men shook hands with each other but did not shake their hands. They had felt slighted and upset. One woman told me she had been so rattled it hurt her performance at the meeting. None of these women had thought to extend their own hands first.

Hugs and Kisses

Social hugging and kissing are much trickier than handshakes. In a business context, greeting someone you know well often involves a gentle hug and light kiss on the cheek. Indeed, in the appropriate circumstances, a gentle hug and social kiss can increase your perceived warmth and social attentiveness, thereby increasing your persuasiveness. But there are pitfalls in this area. When you greet a business colleague you know well and you have hugged and kissed in the past, you should initiate the brief gesture, ending the physical contact relatively quickly. If you have never hugged or kissed this person before, it is up to you to decide whether it is appropriate to do so. This depends on your personality, the personality of the other person, the situation, and the culture of your organization. When in doubt, opt for a good handshake and move on. Of course, if the other person initiates the gesture, smile and make the most of your ability to establish a solid connection.

Listening and Nodding

Women and men tend to listen in different ways. When listening, women tend to lean forward and nod frequently to acknowledge they are paying attention. Men, on the other hand, tend to lean back and are not likely to nod unless they are in agreement with what is being said.

Andie: The different ways in which women and men use head nodding were made crystal clear to me many years ago. As I walked out
of a meeting with Joe, a senior male colleague, he roundly criticized
me for "supporting" the position advanced by the lawyer for the other
side of the deal. I was flabbergasted. I had not said a word in support
of the other side's positions. I had, however, been nodding during the
other side's presentation. I was nodding simply to show I was listening, not that I agreed with what was being said. But my nodding had
confused Joe. He would never have nodded unless he agreed with
what was being said.

Andie's story does not mean that as a woman you should never
nod except when you are in agreement with the speaker. By nodding, you can positively influence another speaker—encouraging her,
engendering hope of agreement, and promoting a positive regard for
yourself. Using head nodding selectively, therefore, is an effective technique for managing the impressions you make. By nodding occasionally when another person is talking, you can build rapport, enhance
trust, and soften nonverbal behavior projecting competence and power.
The key here is to do this occasionally. You never want to look like a
bobblehead doll.

Touching

If, when, and how to touch a person with whom you are interacting in
a business setting may be the trickiest of all nonverbal behavior. Nevertheless, a light touch can be one of the most valuable tools you have for
exhibiting warmth, social sensitivity, and likability.

An appropriate touch in a business context is a brief, light touch
with your hand on another person's arm, shoulder, upper back, or hand.
It is never a touch on the face, head, chest, lower back, or body below the
waist. In fact, some people are fine with a light touch on the arm, but

not of their hand. And, there are people who prefer not to be touched at all. Be on the lookout for nonverbal cues as to the receptivity to touch. But most people, in suitable circumstances, respond positively to being lightly touched; the trick is to know when and how.

Let's look at some interesting examples of the effective use of touch. One researcher intentionally left a coin in a phone booth, waited for the next person to visit the booth, and then asked that person if she or he had found the coin. If the researcher touched that person lightly on the elbow, 96 percent of those asked returned the coin, but if the researcher did not touch the other person when asking about the coin, only 63 percent of the people returned the coin.[4] Another study found that waitresses and waiters who touched the arm or hand of their customers received significantly larger tips than did those who did not.[5]

It is apparent from these studies that touch can be a powerful tool in presenting yourself as a trustworthy and likable person. Nevertheless, you need to be sensitive to context and interpersonal relationships. A pat on a colleague's shoulder as you advise him about a difficult professional problem can be a welcome and reassuring gesture. The same gesture used with a coworker over whom you have just been promoted can be interpreted as condescending and disingenuous. Touch can reinforce your message, but avoid it if it is not fully in sync with your actual feelings.

One of the most valuable ways you can use touch is to soften forceful behavior or get more buy-in to a particularly difficult plan of action. You can use a variety of other nonverbal behavior for the same purposes in such circumstances—pleasant facial expressions, soft voice, inclusive gestures—but a gentle touch might be the most effective technique for increasing the acceptance of your message. A pat on the shoulder, a squeeze of an arm, and a social hug can all express your concern, warmth, and social sensitivity. Likewise, when you ask someone to do something that may be difficult or inconvenient—"I need you to get this done today"—a touch on the shoulder or arm can go a long way toward showing you appreciate the extra effort that will be involved.

Hands and Arms

You want to use your hands and arms to emphasize, clarify, and reinforce what you are saying. For the most part, this will happen naturally if you keep your hands visible and maintain an erect, open posture. We are not fans of prescribing the sorts of hand and arm gestures a woman should use. As long as your gestures are smooth, natural, and not exaggerated, there are many gesture styles that can work quite well. If your attitude is one of confidence and competence, your hand and arm movements should take care of themselves.

If you are not satisfied with your normal hand and arm gestures, watch a half dozen or so TED Talks by different women. Study their gestures and evaluate the effectiveness of their body movements. When you find a style that is particularly appealing and powerful, incorporate some of its elements into your own speaking style. Practice speaking before a full-length mirror (or, better yet, record yourself): watch the way you move, hold yourself, and gesture. If you are unsure of the persuasiveness of your gestures, invite a friend to critique you as you rehearse a prepared speech.

Appearance

Your appearance is probably your single most powerful nonverbal communication tool. We are well aware that the subject of women's appearance is a virtual minefield. From experience, we know that any suggestion we might make about clothing, hairstyle, makeup, and accessories will expose us to charges of sexism, being out of date, undercutting self-expression, destroying authenticity, and worse. Your appearance, however, just like every other aspect of your career behavior, carries positive or negative consequences because of the gender stereotypes and discriminatory biases operating within your organization. As a result, you can get your appearance right or wrong; and to put it bluntly, getting it right helps your career. Therefore, just as with every other aspect of your behavior, to cope effectively with the gender stereotypes associated with appearance, you need to understand these stereotypes and develop techniques for dealing with them.

The double bind with respect to appearance is that a woman who is too attractive risks being thought not serious, lacking in competence, and low in power. On the other hand, a woman whose appearance is judged to be too bland, austere, and unattractive risks being seen as unfeminine, cold, and unlikable. As a result, women pursuing a career need once again to play Goldilocks and get their appearance just right.

Your appearance has a number of components: age, physical characteristics, grooming, dress, and accessories. There is little we can say about the first two but the last three offer a wide variety of possibilities. And it is in this area that many women see advice as intrusive, inappropriate, and a suggestion that they be inauthentic. But when your appearance is that of a person with style, presence, and importance, the people with whom you are interacting are likely to view you as competent as well as socially adept, friendly, and likable.

It is useful to break appearance down into two parts: how your appearance affects the way you think about yourself and how your appearance affects the way other people think about you.

Perhaps the most revealing study about your appearance affecting the way you think about yourself is a 2012 study of the effect of wearing a white lab coat. In the first experiment, half the participants wore a lab coat that they were told was a doctor's jacket. The other half wore their street clothes. Those who wore the white coat made only about half as many errors on a test of selective attention as did those in their street clothes.[6] In the second experiment, all participants wore a white coat but half were told it was a doctor's coat and half were told it was a painter's coat. The group that was told they were wearing a doctor's coat did significantly better on a test for sustained attention than did those who wore an identical coat but had been told it was a painter's coat.[7]

Not surprisingly, these experiments were designed by Adam Galinsky, the social psychologist whose work we used as the basis for much of our discussion of mind priming in chapter 4. Galinsky was looking to determine whether behavior is affected by the symbolic meaning your appearance has for you. What his white coat experiments indicate is that your decisions about your appearance—how you dress, groom, and accessorize—should be dictated by the appearance characteristics you associate with the sort of impression you want to make. The characteristics on which you should focus are not specific items of dress or grooming, such as power suits, short hair, or glamorous makeup, but types of style, such as elegant *or* casual, powerful *or* cheerful, composed *or* relaxed. Once you have done that, you will realize there are a lot of looks that will accomplish your objectives.

Take, for example, three very powerful women who have chosen quite different looks for themselves. Sheryl Sandberg, the COO of Facebook and author of *Lean In,* generally wears form-fitting knits, open necklines, and bright colors. Christine Lagarde, the head of the International Monetary Fund, wears dark, tailored suits that she accessorizes with bright, patterned scarves and an elegant haircut. In contrast to both of these women, Samantha Power, the U.S. ambassador to the United Nations, wears a mishmash of clothes without any apparent consistency.

All three of these women are highly successful, confident, and powerful. Yet, the appearances they have chosen for themselves are very different. And that is our point. In calling attention to these women, we want to emphasize that there is no right way to dress for career success. The way you dress, groom, and accessorize should be guided by the impression you want to make and your own personal comfort in doing so.

Al: Donna is an extraordinarily bright woman who comes across as shy and timid. When she speaks, what she says is always thoughtful, coherent, and articulate, but her delivery is without passion or energy. She always wears pantsuits in dark colors with few accessories. Donna and I were talking one day about self-confidence. She told me she had been a cross-country runner in high school and college, and a good one. When she ran, she said she felt powerful and confident. I asked her whether there had been any recent situations in which she felt the way she did when she was running. To my surprise, she said

(Continued)

she had felt that way at her sister's wedding when she wore a colorful tailored dress. So I stuck my neck out and asked her if she ever wore skirts or dresses to the office. She said, no, she had been told that serious women wore pants in dark colors without jewelry. I let the subject drop.

About a month later, I found an opportunity to say something to Donna about another woman's presentation: "Did you see Claire's presentation? Do you think she hurt her effectiveness by wearing an orange dress?" This really caught her off guard. "No" was her reply. Not long after that, I noticed Donna was wearing a dress. She confidently handled a difficult exchange in a meeting that same day, so I made it a point to compliment her, not on her appearance, but on her increased confidence. She beamed. Neither one of us mentioned her dress. Donna now varies her wardrobe style, and her clothes are more colorful. Her timidness is by no means completely gone, but her increased confidence is obvious.

We have not found any specific rules for the look women should strive for in pursuing career success, but we offer three general observations:

1. No two women are alike in their appearance objectives. What works for a female coworker may be entirely wrong for you.
2. The look with which you are comfortable will depend in large part on your industry, customers/clients, geographic location, and the culture of your organization. What works in Silicon Valley is unlikely to work on Wall Street.
3. Your appearance objective, similar to your objective with respect to the rest of your nonverbal behavior, is to get the job done. You need to act in ways that facilitate your ability to accomplish the tasks and meet the challenges you face. The same is true with your appearance: you need to present yourself as someone capable of accomplishing what needs to be done to sell the product, close the deal, design the building, lead the project, or whatever it is you are expected to do.

Turning to the way your appearance affects how other people regard you, your objective should be to make an impression as the sort of woman you want to be perceived to be. This means you need to treat your physical appearance just as seriously as you treat all other aspects of your communication. Once you are clear about the message you want to send about your seriousness, ambition, self-confidence, competence, and yes, sexuality, then you need to figure out how to dress accordingly. The impression you want to make will differ based on setting, objectives, and interpersonal relationships. One obvious clue is to observe how others in your industry or organization dress and then decide if you want to fit in or stand out.[8]

KEY TAKEAWAYS

■ Obtain an accurate picture of your characteristic nonverbal behavior. Approach this in three ways: self-monitoring, directly observing yourself, and enlisting other people to critique your nonverbal behavior. Try to use all three approaches to come to an understanding of the type of person your nonverbal behavior reveals you to be.

■ Find role models. Carefully observe the nonverbal behavior of women you admire who have influence, trust, and respect. Create a list of nonverbal traits you find most attractive and influential, and start incorporating them into your own nonverbal behavior.

■ Guard against nonverbal behavior that is inconsistent with the message you are working to deliver. Watch a recording of yourself to see whether your behavior is in sync with your intended message.

■ Use positive nonverbal behavior that shows agentic traits: stand tall, use space, and gesture expansively. But also consciously project the communal traits of warmth, inclusivity, and likability.

■ Smile frequently, but only when appropriate.

■ If your nonverbal behavior exhibits confidence, competence, power, *and* warmth, you will be seen as a leader. Your physical stature does not matter; it is all about your behavior.[9]

■ Dress the part. Your appearance gives an impression of the sort of woman you are, signaling your ambition, power, competence, and energy. Treat your physical appearance as seriously as you treat all other aspects of your nonverbal communication.

6

Spoken and Written Behavior

When you communicate in an articulate, engaging, and friendly way, other people enjoy communicating with you. More significantly, when you can communicate in this way, you are able to avoid the adverse consequences of the double binds you face because of the gender stereotypes in your workplace. By being able to speak and write with ease and grace, you can effectively present yourself and your ideas without triggering the negative reactions that women so frequently encounter when they seek to demonstrate their leadership ability. In this chapter, we discuss some simple techniques you can use to enhance your ability to speak and write with both strength and warmth. We also identify some communication patterns you should avoid because they are likely to provoke negative impressions.

YOUR VOICE

Your voice is a key component of your ability to present yourself as an energetic leader, capable problem solver, and effective negotiator. Yet the stereotypes associated with women's voices often make this difficult. Consider the voices and speech patterns of two iconic women of the twentieth century: Marilyn Monroe and Margaret Thatcher. Monroe's trademark whispering, pleading, singsong voice contributed to her image as sexy, unintelligent, submissive, and in need of male protection. By contrast, Thatcher's steady pitch, calculated volume shifts, and use of silences for emphasis marked her as a strong, authoritative, and capable leader. Neither of these impressions fully reflected these women's actual personalities, but stereotypes are not about nuanced and accurate judgments. When you speak, your audience forms an impression of you that is likely to be one-dimensional. Your goal, therefore, is to use a speaking style that encourages others to form an impression of you as capable, confident, and approachable.

Among the verbal techniques you can use to project authority and warmth are a steady tempo, moments of silence, varied volume, and controlled pitch. Louder, more fluent voices stereotypically communicate confidence and are heard as more persuasive than high-pitched, discordant ones. Regardless of the brilliance of the substantive content of what you are saying, if your speech is difficult for others to hear, halting, involves frequent slips of the tongue, has little variation in volume, frequent repetitions, and vocalized pauses, you will find it difficult to make an impression as competent and persuasive.

Tempo

Your goal should be to speak at a steady, moderate pace (neither slow nor rushed). When the people to whom you are talking find your speech's tempo pleasant and easy to listen to, you are more likely to make an impression of knowing what you are talking about. Keep in mind that if you talk too fast, you will appear excited, nervous, or uncomfortable, and other people's impressions of your competence will go down.[1] On the other hand, if you speak too slowly, you run the risk of boring your listeners or giving a Marilyn Monroe impression: seductive but not very bright.

We have found three techniques particularly effective in helping women speak at an appropriate speed.

1. Match your tempo to that of the people with whom you are speaking. By putting yourself in sync with others, you will increase your persuasiveness and enhance your impression as someone who is approachable and socially sensitive.

2. Rehearse a speech with a stopwatch in your hand. A good rule of thumb is to speak at between 140 and 165 words per minute. At this pace, you can comfortably make occasional tempo changes and pause to emphasize your points.
3. Read a book out loud while listening to a professional reader on an audiobook.
4. Watch the YouTube video of Angelina Jolie speaking at the 2009 World Refugee Day to hear a comfortable conversational speaker.[2]

Your pace, of course, should depend on the content and context of your topic. When introducing a new and complex topic, your pace should be slower than it would be for a subject familiar to your listeners.

Moments of Silence

Pauses, that is, moments of complete silence, are an effective way for you to emphasize key points and underscore the importance of your message. There are various ways you can do this. When you reach a break between your ideas you can take a sip of water, look around at your listeners, or glance down at your papers. Whatever technique allows you to pause comfortably is fine. The point is to give your listeners time to absorb one idea before you present the next, or to appreciate fully the importance of a point you have just made, or for you to pique their interest in what you will say next. Imagine a speaker saying, "That project was the most..." then pausing. You would be keen to know what is coming next and, therefore, be paying close attention. Pauses are particularly effective between strong parallels ("of the people...by the people...for the people"), after someone asks you a question, and at the beginning and end of your presentation.

As powerful as a moment of silence can be, many women are reluctant to pause while they are speaking for fear they will be interrupted and lose the floor. In chapter 8, we discuss techniques for holding the floor, so don't let this fear stop you from using controlled silences. When you have a group's attention, you are on stage. This is an opportunity to display your competence, mastery of the material, and the importance of your message. Short silences help you do this because they convey your power and confidence without your appearing in any way aggressive or intimidating.

Tone

You convey a great deal about how you are feeling by your tone of voice. Common voice tones include frustration, anger, whining, sarcasm, pleading, firmness, friendliness, humor, pleasure, warmth, submissiveness, superiority, excitement, happiness, and sadness. When you have a warm, friendly tone of voice, you make an impression of being approachable and likable, someone your listeners can trust and rely on. If your tone is pleading or submissive, you make an impression as someone to whom they don't need to pay close attention. The important point is to be aware of your tone of voice and to be certain that it reinforces your substantive message—and does not convey something about your feelings that you don't want to reveal.

Volume

Your speech volume can be tricky to get right. If you speak too loudly, you can be seen as aggressive. If you speak too softly, you can be seen as without power, competence, or confidence. One technique you can use to get your volume right is to take your cue from the volume at which the people with whom you are interacting are speaking. Another technique is to record yourself speaking at different volume levels until you find one you believe is appropriate and with which you are comfortable— loud enough so everyone in a medium-sized conference room can hear you without straining, but not so loud that other people find it unpleasant to listen to you. Whatever your normal or regular volume level, you should vary it; without such variations, you can come off as monotonous and boring. Increase your volume to emphasize a point or focus your listener's attention, and decrease your volume to draw your listeners in and build anticipation. Persuasive speech holds people's interest so they pay attention to what you are saying. By varying the volume at which you are speaking, you can do this in a particularly effective way.

Pitch

Deeper, lower-pitched voices are stereotypically thought to be more authoritative, powerful, and persuasive than higher-pitched voices. Women typically have higher-pitched voices than men, and as a result men's voices are often thought to be "better" because they are more authoritative and knowledgeable than women's. It is very difficult to change the pitch of your voice, and we generally advise women to speak with their natural voices. You should, however, be conscious of your pitch, try to stay away from your highest registers, and keep your pitch as low as you can comfortably. If your vocal pitch really bothers you, however, there are voice coaches who can help.

Al: Susan is an architect and a very good one. She is also a very small woman with a youthful face. She has a high-pitched voice and used to speak frequently in her higher vocal registers. Susan told me that early in her career she often failed to win major projects because she was unable to present herself as forceful and capable of leading a large team. She knew she could not change her size or facial appearance, but she thought she could change her voice. She hired a voice coach who, over the course of more than a year, helped her learn to speak in a lower register by relaxing her vocal chords and imagining her voice coming from down deep in her throat. Over time, her voice became noticeably lower and deeper. Susan told me that with more confidence in the power of her speaking ability she was more effective in presenting herself as a competent, capable architect. She started to be awarded more projects, and she is now one of the most sought-after architects in her city.

Range

Your voice range is the full span of the high and low notes that your voice can reach when speaking or singing. Women's voices tend to start at a higher pitch than men's and to have a larger overall range. Because of their wider vocal range, women can often unconsciously play into the traditional gender stereotype that women are emotional.

Andie: Over the years, I've frequently attended meetings with male colleagues or clients who later referred to a woman at the meeting as emotional, excited, or even irrational. I had been at those same meetings, but typically I hadn't seen or heard women being in any way emotional. What I had heard was a woman using her full vocal range as she spoke. When I would ask my colleagues and clients why they thought this or that woman was emotional, they typically said something like, "Didn't you hear her voice? She was out of control." They assumed that a woman's variation in the pitch of her voice meant she was highly emotional.

Because of the "women are emotional" stereotype, you should be alert to your pitch variations. Don't use a singsongy voice and don't drift off into your highest register unless you want to speak up there.

UNDESIRABLE SPEECH PATTERNS

The substantive content of what you have to say can be overshadowed by the way you say it. As a result, you want to be alert to types of speech or particular speech patterns that give an impression you are pretentious, passive, or incompetent. Effective impression management depends on banishing these sorts of verbal behavior from your speech repertoire.

Vocal Fry

Vocal fry involves speaking in the lowest possible vocal range with a pronounced croaking or guttural use of the vocal cords. When people use vocal fry, they often extend the pronunciation of words by elongating particular syllables. The Kardashians use vocal fry. Both Jill Abramson, former editor-in-chief of the *New York Times*, and George

W. Bush have used vocal fry during public speaking engagements.[3] But only Abramson's, not Bush's, voice was labeled as "unusual" by a linguistic researcher.[4]

Our advice about vocal fry is simple, if a little stuffy: don't use it. The problem with vocal fry is that using this speaking style risks you being seen as annoying, pretentious, bored, lazy, or immature.

If you are a young woman at the beginning of your career, you already face biases based on your age, experience, and gender. Don't burden yourself further by using a speaking technique that your male superiors (and some of your female ones, too) are likely to find off-putting or worse.

Uptalk

When you ask a question, your sentence typically ends with a rising intonation. Uptalk (or upspeak) is using a rising intonation when you are making a declaratory statement. Valley Girls popularized uptalk in the 1980s. Women tend to use uptalk because they don't want to be seen as giving the final word or asserting power, or they want to show solidarity with a particular group of people. Whatever the reason for using uptalk, it is a speech pattern that you should generally avoid. Older business and professional people are likely to find uptalk to be a sign that you lack competence, power, and self-confidence.

There may be occasions on which you can use uptalk to show your softer, more communal characteristics. Uptalk can be an effective technique, for example, when you want to appear to be particularly inclusive or want to demonstrate you are fully engaged with the group in a highly cooperative task. But use uptalk carefully. In the wrong situations, it can mark you as indecisive, lacking in confidence, and timid.

Andie: Madison is a very successful surgeon who used uptalk, in her words, "to great success throughout college." But when she got to medical school, she found that her uptalk was confusing other people, particularly the senior doctors and patients. When she would

(Continued)

end her instructions with a rising inflection, she was not making the positive impression she wanted. When she told her patients to "Take two tablets in the morning?" they were puzzled. If Madison asked for a scalpel in surgery, she did not want her surgical team wondering if she really wanted a scalpel or their opinion about whether a scalpel was the appropriate tool. So Madison started breaking her habit of uptalk. It took time and a lot of practice, but Madison has stopped her uptalk, and she tells me it has greatly improved her communication with her patients and her team in the hospital.

Tag Questions

Tag questions (or tail questions) turn declaratory statements into questions by tagging a superfluous question onto the end. Examples of this practice are:

- "That's a good idea don't you think?"
- "The purchase orders need to be signed by noon don't they?"
- "The customer needs the product tomorrow do you agree?"

Tag questions can be annoying and confusing and should generally be avoided. They suggest you are unsure of your conclusion or need someone to confirm it for you. Phrases such as "Isn't it?," "Don't you agree?," "You know?," "Haven't we?," "Okay?," and "Right?" reduce the force of your statements and give the impression you lack confidence. Moreover, because tag questions suggest tentativeness, you can come across as uncertain, poorly prepared, or lacking a take-charge attitude.

Because tag questions, like uptalk, suggest inclusiveness and a rejection of power, there are situations in which you might want to use them to show you are approachable and want others to speak up and join the discussion. In other words, when your objective is to present the communal and welcoming side of your personality, tag questions can be useful. If you are fully aware of what you are doing and believe that a tag question will lead to a better overall result, by all means use it. Otherwise, you would be well advised to avoid it.

Indirectness

In a familiar double bind, if a woman behaves decisively, for example, by arguing vigorously for her point of view, the people with whom she is dealing may find her overly agentic, lacking in warmth, and decidedly unlikable. On the other hand, if she behaves deferentially and is not proactive, she may come across as communal and likable but not a leader. Because of this dilemma, women frequently use indirection in an attempt to state their position without coming off as bossy, strident, or aggressive. Most of the time, however, indirection is a bad idea. You are obscuring your ideas and instructions. Take, for example, the following:

- "Do you think it is too hot in here?"
- "You might want to think about the XYZ line of cases."
- "It might be easier if we lived closer to X."
- "Would you have time to work on the Y project?"

You generally want to avoid ambiguity, and indirection of this sort is a rich source of ambiguity.

In addition, indirection won't get you out of the too assertive/too weak double bind. Instead, it creates the impression you lack confidence and certainty as to what you want. You will be far more effective in navigating this double bind if you are able to project both agentic *and* communal characteristics. Speak clearly and directly, but also smile, maintain a pleasant expression, express warmth, and gesture in welcoming and inclusive ways. Indirection is a losing verbal style. As the saying goes, say what you mean and mean what you say.

UNDESIRABLE WORDS AND PHRASES

There are a number of commonplace words and phrases that may seem innocuous but that severely undermine the effectiveness of your communication.

"Like"

The use of "like" in grammatically superfluous ways has become ubiquitous, at least among young women and girls. All too often we hear phrases such as, "We, like, rock," "It's, like, an awesome dress," "Is this, like, a necessary thing to do?," and "You, like, like that guy?" We are aware that some linguists think that the grammatically unnecessary "like" is used as a tool for building relationships and is a genuine linguistic innovation. Nevertheless, we have not been able to find a single example of the grammatically superfluous use of "like" by a Fortune 500 CEO, a senior academic over age forty-five, or a general in the U.S. military. Consequently, if you frequently add superfluous "likes" to your sentences, you risk your verbal behavior being regarded as distracting, even irritating. The grammatically unnecessary use of the word "likes" will not advance your effort to present yourself as mature, forceful, and competent.

Self-Deprecation

Women often undermine their own credibility by depreciating the value or relevance of their own ideas. Far too frequently women in business settings use phrases such as the following:

- "I may be off base here, but..."
- "I don't know if this is helpful, but..."
- "Maybe I'm wrong about this, but..."
- "I'm not an expert, but..."

This sort of self-deprecation in all likelihood comes from a woman's concern that she not be viewed as bossy or too assertive. But it is a linguistic habit that makes you look weak, tentative, and not like a leader. You can break this habit by listening to yourself—self-monitoring—and choosing what you say for maximum impact.

"You Know"

The phrase "you know" is a filler phrase or verbal tic similar to "um," "er," "ah," "basically," "I mean," "okay," "so," and "etcetera, etcetera." Most people use filler words and phrases from time to time, but there is a reason that professional speakers are trained to avoid them. Filler words and phrases undercut your ability to project an image of competence, authority, and confidence. Take, for example, Caroline Kennedy. When Kennedy was seeking to be appointed to the U.S. Senate in 2008, she was asked by the *New York Daily News* whether President George W. Bush's tax cuts for the wealthy should be repealed. Kennedy replied, "Well, you know, that's something, obviously, that, you know, in principle and in the campaign, you know, I think that, um, the tax cuts, you know, were expiring and needed to be repealed." In her thirty-minute interview with the *Daily News*, Kennedy used the phrase "you know" more than two hundred times.[5] Because of this, she came across as inexperienced, uncertain, and lacking both knowledge and confidence. Not surprisingly, she wasn't appointed to the Senate.

If your verbal communication regularly includes "you knows" or other filler words or phrases, you should work hard to clean them out. Two techniques we have found helpful are pausing whenever you catch yourself about to use a filler word and memorizing and then reciting fairly lengthy passages. One way or another, however, "you know" needs to go.

"Just"

Women tend to say "just" more frequently than men do, and it is another word that sounds weak, submissive, and rarely adds anything to a statement. Questions using "just" mark you as tentative and lacking in confidence.

- "Do you have just a minute?"
- "Can we just stop to just think about this?"

A former Google and Apple executive recently criticized women's use of "just." She called it a child word, one that puts the other person in the position of the parent; it conveys a subtle message of subordination, deference, and self-effacement. When you use "just" in a grammatically superfluous way, you weaken and confuse your message.[6]

"I'm Sorry"

Women say "I'm sorry" far too frequently when they are not apologizing for something they have done, but merely to express concern or sympathy, to show solidarity, or to build and retain relationships.[7]

- He says, "It's raining"; she says, "I'm sorry."
- He says, "Our client is upset"; she says, "I'm sorry."
- He says, "We lost the customer"; she says, "I'm sorry."
- He says, "My presentation didn't go well"; she says, "I'm sorry."

The "he" in these examples could be replaced by a "she," but the "she" could not realistically be replaced by a "he." Men typically don't say "I'm sorry" as a relationship builder. Men only say "I'm sorry" when they have committed an actual mistake or transgression—and not always then.

However valuable the phrase "I'm sorry" may be in your personal life, it is a very dangerous one in your career life. Saying "I'm sorry" when you have done nothing wrong suggests you are responsible in some way for whatever has happened. Did you have something to do with that lost customer or unfavorable presentation?

A woman might also use "I'm sorry" when making a request—"I'm sorry, but would you mind answering a few questions?"—to avoid being seen as bossy or aggressive. Using "I'm sorry" in this way is, then, an attempt to appear more accessible, less threatening, and more likable. But being seen as more likable does you no good in your career if you are also seen as defensive or unsure of yourself. Apologizing or taking responsibility for things that aren't your fault undermines your credibility. As a strong, confident woman, you will often need to find a way to soften your image so you are not perceived as rude, abrasive, or pushy. But saying "I'm sorry" is not the way to accomplish this.

"FEEL"

Another enemy that will prevent you from making an impression as forceful, direct, and competent is the use of emotional language. Think about the impression you would make with the following statements:

- "I feel good about the design development."
- "How do you feel about the company's paying so much for that property?"
- "What's your feeling about this undertaking?"
- "I don't feel good about this acquisition."
- "How do you feel about the other side's arguments?

All of these statements and questions are about emotions, not facts or results. No one cares about how you *feel* about the decision; they want to know what you *think* about it. Emotion-based language plays directly into the widely held gender stereotype that women are emotional and not decisive, touchy-feely, not factual.

Emotional language should have a very limited role in your workplace vocabulary. You should use precise action verbs when you express your ideas or ask questions. Stay away from vague emotional verbs such as "feel," "want," and "need." You should talk (and think) about the issues you face in your workplace in a direct, careful, logical manner. You are after clarity not emotion, strength not needing, conciseness not effusiveness.

"I"

Starting your sentences with "I" is similar to using emotional language. The problem should be apparent from statements such as the following:

- "I believe this plan is a bad one."
- "I think our company should move forward with this deal."
- "I like the way the new communication system works."
- "I wonder if we could talk about the budget."

When you begin a sentence with "I," the expectation is that the sentence will be about you. But these statements are not about you; they are about the idea, the company, and the communication system. Not only do "I" statements confuse your listeners, they can be discounted as being merely the way *you* see things.

If you think the plan is a bad one say, "This plan is bad because…" You are not important; your ideas, skills, and persuasive power are the important things here. Put them on display and get the "I" off stage. In fact, unless you are indeed talking about yourself, drop the use of "I" altogether. In most career contexts—self-evaluations and claiming credit for your successes are obvious exceptions—your language will be more forceful, active, credible, intelligent, and professional if you never use "I."

WRITTEN (MOSTLY ELECTRONIC) COMMUNICATION

All of the words and phrases you should avoid when speaking you should also avoid when you are writing. As organizations rely more and more on electronic communication—e-mail, text, instant messaging, Twitter, Facebook, and other social media—you need to be increasingly sensitive to the impression you are making with your written words. You can encounter double binds in written communications just as you can in spoken communications. Therefore, many of the principles of attuned gender communication are as relevant when you are writing as they are when you are speaking.

From the perspective of gender stereotypes, electronic communication has drawbacks and advantages for a woman. The drawbacks all concern the risk your message will be misunderstood. Because so much of communication is nonverbal, it is difficult, if not impossible, to electronically convey humor, sarcasm, irony, exaggeration, skepticism, disapproval, or deep emotion. This is, of course, also true for traditional business communication, but written business communication is generally in the form of letters that are routinized and formal. But because electronic communication is much more common and informal, the risks of it being misunderstood are much greater.

On the other hand, the advantage of electronic communication is that it significantly limits the possibility of discriminatory behavior directed against a woman. This is because when using e-mail or texting, people generally take turns, and a man will find it difficult to interrupt a woman or dominate the discussion. A woman, thus, has an opportunity to present her ideas at the length and in the way she wants.

Keep in mind that electronic communication is forever, so you never want to post anything online or write anything in an e-mail that you would not want your current or future employers to see. Don't rely on privacy settings; they don't always work the way you assume they do. Anything potentially embarrassing or that reflects badly on you does not belong in an e-mail or posted on the Internet. And remember, the information on your business computer and smartphone belongs to (and can be accessed at any time by) your employer.

When working with senior colleagues, don't expect them to conform to your preferred way of communicating. If the style of your senior colleagues is face-to-face meetings, carefully consider the appropriateness of asking to call in to a meeting or participate by Skype. If they e-mail but never text, don't attempt to communicate with them by text. And if they communicate with customers only by phone and formal written communication, don't send e-mails. Many younger employees avoid the phone and in-office visits because they do not want to intrude on others. Unless you have been told by a senior colleague to avoid these communication methods, it is best to use them.

> *AI:* Doreen asked a new designer at her marketing firm to set up a call with a client later that day. At about 2 p.m., Doreen realized she had not heard back from the designer about the call. Doreen walked to the designer's desk and asked if the call had been scheduled. She was told, "I don't know, I never heard back from my e-mail." Doreen then asked, "Did you follow up with a call?" The designer's response was, "A telephone call? I never thought of that."

Communication patterns, like appropriate work attire, are changing. But your objective is to be noticed as someone ready to move up in *your* organization. So look up, and follow the communication practices used by your senior colleagues.

KEY TAKEAWAYS

■ Use your voice to create the impression you want. The way you speak can play a far more important role in the impressions you make on other people than the actual substance of your ideas and opinions.

■ Make your verbal behavior powerful. Use relaxed, deep breaths to project your words and speak with power; use your diaphragm, lungs, mouth, and nose when you speak; open your mouth and pronounce your words clearly; pause at key moments, such as just before or right after an important point.

■ Keep a steady vocal pitch while shifting between louder and softer volumes. Use inflections to emphasize your points, use strategic pauses, and avoid long speech sequences in your highest voice range.

■ If you are feeling anxious or worried, make a special effort to keep your tone of voice even and your volume moderate. You want your listeners to focus on the content of your message without being distracted by emotional inflections.

■ Keep your speaking speed under control. Speak at a comfortable and conversational rate.

■ Be conscious of your tone of voice. You generally want it to be pleasant and warm, but you need to be sure your tone is forceful and confident when needed. Your tone should never be pleading or suggest submissiveness. A sarcastic tone can turn off your listeners and reveal emotions you are trying to hide. To help you sound confident, relax your upper body and shoulders.

■ Mind priming can positively affect your voice, so do a mind priming exercise before an important conversation.

■ If you don't know what vocal fry sounds like, visit YouTube and watch a video about vocal fry or "The Kardashians Talk Back to Tweets."[8]

■ Avoid uptalk, a passive voice, hedges, and tag questions that make you sound uncertain about your ideas, positions, and beliefs. Weak spoken or written language is weak, and you should avoid it, period.

■ Speak directly and avoid ambiguity. Make your points clearly. Speaking indirectly confuses your listeners and hurts your credibility.

■ Avoid self-deprecating statements such as "I may be off base."

■ Learn to say "I'm sorry" only when you have something to apologize for, not to connect with other people or water down your statements and requests. Watch how comedian Amy Schumer handled the "I'm sorry" issue in a recent sketch linked to the article "Try This Experiment If You Say 'Sorry' Too Much."[9]

■ Say what you mean. Be sure there are no contradictions between the words you use and the verbal and nonverbal messages you are sending.

■ Listen to women you respect in the news and on the Internet. Watch a few TED Talks. Try to mimic their speaking styles. Try this while looking in a mirror or by recording yourself.

■ If your language is strong, your pace and volume appropriate, and your tone confident, even a thin, small voice can demonstrate power.

■ Avoid emotional words and phrases such as "I feel," "My gut tells me," and "I have a good sense for this." It is your ideas that are important, not your feelings.

■ Write professionally. When sending a written or electronic communication, use full sentences, typically without abbreviations or emoticons.

■ Electronic communications offer you the opportunity to think through your comments and responses. Take advantage of this opportunity. When speaking directly to someone, your verbal and nonverbal behavior help to ensure that your meaning and intent are clear. In an e-mail, you only have the written words. So write your e-mails carefully, however casual they are meant to be.

PART IV

Communicating in Difficult Situations

7

Difficult and Tricky Interactions

Gender stereotypes often lead women and men to interpret their interactions very differently. When this happens at work, it is often the woman who ends up disadvantaged, confused, and intimidated. Situations as common as getting an assignment, presenting the results of a project, and giving or receiving feedback can all result in misunderstandings and strained business relations. One-on-one personal interactions carry the same risks. Situations ranging from the straightforward—saying no, apologizing, and handling compliments—to the decidedly non-straightforward—unwanted sexual advances, unflattering rumors, and intrusive prying into one's private life can all pose career dangers.

In this chapter we identify some potentially difficult and tricky interactions, discuss the problems that gender stereotypes can cause in these situations, and offer attuned gender communication techniques to prevent or ameliorate these difficulties.

GIVING AND ACCEPTING ASSIGNMENTS

Women and men often give out and accept assignments in different ways. For example, a woman might provide an assignment by giving instructions and directions in an indirect way, almost as if she were making a suggestion. Thus, a woman might say something like, "It might be helpful to contact the customer to learn," "You might want to consider the XYZ line of cases," or "Would you be available to help me with the ABC project?" A man in a similar situation is likely to be far more direct, saying something like, "I want you to call the customer tomorrow," "You should carefully review the XYZ line of cases," or "I want you on the ABC project next week."

We suspect that when a woman gives an assignment in this indirect, "I'm only making a suggestion" way, she wants to avoid appearing to be giving a direct order, or she wants the person receiving the assignment to feel a sense of joint ownership of the project. These are understandable objectives, but a person using indirection runs the risk of appearing weak and uncertain. If a woman gives an assignment to a man in an indirect way, she may find he has misinterpreted her statements as suggestions, so he fails to do the assignment in the way she wanted. He might decide *not* to call the customer or *not* to include an analysis of the XYZ line of cases. When this happens, she is likely to get angry and criticize him because she had "told" him to call the customer or analyze the XYZ line of cases. He, in turn, will feel unfairly treated—after all, she only made a suggestion. He complains about her to their colleagues: "She doesn't know what she wants." For her part, she is likely to criticize him as being inattentive and not very bright. What started as a straightforward assignment has now turned into a disaster. And, the disaster started because she didn't want to be seen as bossy.

Giving an assignment is not the time to build camaraderie or create a sense of shared ownership. At *this* time, you need to be explicit and leave no ambiguity about what you want and when you want it. As the project proceeds, you can provide a sense of inclusiveness.

Women and men can also communicate differently when receiving an assignment. A woman is likely to ask a lot of questions when she gets the project: "Should I call the customer directly?" "Do you want more or less?" "Are you interested in this or that?" "When do you need my answers?" In contrast, a man is much more likely to accept the assignment immediately, saying something like, "I've got it. I'll get right on it." He wants to appear independent and in control; she wants to be sure she gets it right.[1]

In getting an assignment, you want to make two impressions: one at the time you accept it and the second at the time you complete it. When you get the assignment, you want to come across as a confident and proactive problem solver. Don't ask questions because you are nervous, want to make a connection, or want to appear interested. Ask the questions essential for understanding the assignment, and hold the rest of your questions until you can ask them in a concise, focused, knowledgeable, and organized way. When the assignment is complete, you want to be seen as a competent, efficient, and highly skilled worker. If you fail to make the right impression when accepting an assignment, it will be very difficult to effectively make a positive impression when you complete the assignment.

FEEDBACK AND CRITICISM

Women often encounter the same sorts of problems in giving and getting feedback and criticism as they do in giving and getting assignments. In giving feedback, for example, many woman bury their criticism in positive comments; they don't want to damage their relationship with the other person. A female supervisor might say to a male subordinate something like, "You really handled X great, and you should be very proud of that. But Y is not up to my standards." She may think that he will understand that the important part of her feedback was about his poor performance with respect to Y. The man, however, may hear how great he did with X and discount her problem with Y. Or, he might just think she does not know what she wants and dismiss the criticism outright. If you find yourself tempted to sugarcoat criticism, ask yourself whether there is any possibility you might be misunderstood. If there is, drop the sugar and give the vinegar straight.

Feedback and criticism are meant to change behavior; therefore, give them directly, firmly, and unambiguously. Focus on the problem or inadequacy—not on the person who is being criticized. Three key objectives in giving feedback or criticism are clarity, neutrality, and temperance. Clarity requires you to speak in direct statements that are free of ambiguity and euphemisms. Neutrality requires you to maintain verbal and nonverbal behavior without emotion. And, temperance requires you to remain calm, even if you are challenged.[2] Provide specific suggestions for improvements going forward, offer an opportunity for questions and discussion, and then move on. You want to use attuned gender communication to avoid coming off as harsh, stern, cold, or unsympathetic.

When you are receiving feedback or criticism, keep a few important points in mind:

- Don't get emotional. No crying, no anger, no wringing of hands, no expressions of despair. These reactions play directly into negative gender stereotypes of women as emotional, weak, and vulnerable. If you might not be able to remain calm after what you have been told, excuse yourself and only return to the discussion when you are certain you can remain calm. You want all the constructive feedback and criticism you can get, but if you react emotionally, your supervisors are likely to go soft on you when talking with you, not wanting to deal with an emotional woman.

- Don't get defensive. Research shows that women are far more likely than men to take criticism of their work product personally, as an attack on them as human beings. Criticism isn't (or shouldn't be) a personal attack. If you react as though it defines you as a person, you appear as insecure and weak. Treat criticism as a learning opportunity, not an exposure of your weaknesses as a person.

- Don't grovel and apologize excessively. Acknowledge what you did or failed to do, say you're sorry, ask whatever questions you need to ask, and leave it at that. Don't wallow in regret and self-reproach. What's done is done. You want to make an impression that you are taking the criticism to heart and improving as a result, but not remaining stuck on the past.

- Don't make excuses. You may feel you have a perfectly reasonable explanation for why the project didn't meet your supervisor's expectations: you were working on another deal; your mother got sick; you misunderstood the assignment; you accidentally deleted your first draft and had to start all over at the eleventh hour, or whatever. Don't go there.

■ Don't leave the discussion without fully understanding what you need to do so you do not make the same mistakes again. You don't want to ask more questions than are necessary, but you need to ask enough questions to know what was expected of you and what you failed to deliver.

SAYING NO

Some things should be easy for you to say no to: unwelcome sexual requests, criminal and unethical proposals, and activities that pose a high degree of risk to yourself or others. There are other situations that will come up in the course of your career, however, in which it may not be easy to refuse or it is unclear whether you should (or wisely can) say yes or no. We have found three specific situations that pose the greatest difficulties for women in this regard: (1) requests to perform a task or take on a project that *will not* contribute in a meaningful way to advancing your career; (2) requests to perform a task or take on a project that *will* clearly advance your career but which come at a time when you are already very busy; and (3) requests you receive to change your job position within your organization when the career implications of this change are unclear.

You might not see these situations as having much, if anything, to do with gender stereotypes or communicating in ways to avoid gender bias. But your willingness to say no in these situations has everything to do with gender stereotypes. Women are expected to say yes to requests because saying yes is the communal and friendly thing to do. And women want to be liked. Indeed, studies show women say no far less often than do men.[3] For this reason, we believe women are overwhelmingly asked more often than men to staff the administrative and social committees, to take on more than they should, and to perform the bulk of the noncore functions of the business. And women say yes far too often. As a result, women are often stuck in dead-end positions and frustrated by their inability to attain the key positions they desire.

Andie: Helen was a principal at a major consulting firm. She came to me for advice when she realized her compensation was substantially lower than that of her male counterparts. She believed she was doing everything right and could not understand how or why this compensation disparity existed. As I talked with Helen, this is the story that emerged: she is a Hispanic woman and is asked frequently by her firm to speak before various Hispanic groups and audiences with high Hispanic attendance. Her senior colleagues ask her to accompany them on client pitches where her Spanish-language skills are a valuable selling point. Helen recruits for the firm at a dozen business schools in an effort to attract more Hispanics; she serves on her firm's diversity committee; and she is responsible for developing and presenting cultural diversity awareness programs for her colleagues. When I asked to see a record of her hours spent on client projects and fees collected from clients she had originated, both these numbers were well below where they should have been for someone at her seniority level.

You hardly needed to be a rocket scientist to figure out Helen's problem. So I started talking to her about saying no. She stopped going on client pitches with other consultants unless she was going to get a share of the billing credit, she stopped participating in recruiting events, and she ended her diversity committee involvement. She began asking the senior consultants for more work, and she started making client pitches on her own, making use of her extensive network of important and influential Hispanic businesspeople.

Helen encountered a great deal of pushback at first: "We need you to continue to do this," "The firm depends on you," and "You are the only one who can do this." But once her new pattern was established, and she was behaving the same way as the other principals in the firm, she stopped being asked to do these "special things" and started being asked to do real work. It took a full year, but Helen's compensation went up markedly, and it has continued to increase. She is now on track to be made a managing director in the next promotion cycle. When I last spoke with Helen, she said to me, "I thought I was expected to say yes. When I did, people always said thank you and told me how great I was. But it was only when I started saying no that my career took off and I began to be recognized as a valuable member of the team."

When you receive a request to do something that "doesn't count," you need to think about several things before saying yes or no. First, where are you in your career? Whether you are just starting out or well established makes a difference in your ability to say no. If you have been with your company for less than a year or two and your boss asks you to take on a noncore project, the request is not likely to be a request, but an assignment. On the other hand, if you are a fully functioning member of a team with solid accomplishments behind you, you have considerably more flexibility about saying no. In either situation, however, the essential question is whether saying yes will help you be successful in your organization. Consider whether saying yes will be useful for your career advancement, provide you with experiences to develop essential job skills, or be personally fulfilling. Unless you answer yes to at least one of these questions, you need to think seriously about saying no.

Second, what time commitment would be involved? Will it take you away from or disrupt your other responsibilities? Will it reduce the time you spend on things for yourself or time with your friends and family? Depending on who asks, your position in the organization, and the strategic importance for your career of accepting the request, you may conclude you need to take on the project even if it means significantly longer hours on the job and less time for yourself and your family.

Third, how many other noncore projects are you already handling? If these noncore projects are fairly distributed around your organization, you need to handle your appropriate share. But if these projects are going disproportionately to women or to you in particular because you are so good at them, it is time to start saying no.

But what about requests to handle essential or core projects, such as handling a new client project, supervising more customer accounts, participating on a key governance committee, or serving on a product development team? The issues here are far more straightforward than with noncore projects, but you must still consider your position in the organization and who is asking. Beyond that, there are basically only two issues to consider: Can you accept this assignment without your other work suffering? And, will accepting the assignment mean you cannot spend the time you want on yourself or with your family? If your answer to the first question is no, you would be ill advised to accept the assignment. When the quality of your work declines or you start missing deadlines, your reputation within your organization can quickly deteriorate and it may be very hard to recover it.

On the other hand, if it is not a question of your work quality but your time for yourself or with your family, you need to consider how long this period of shortened personal time will last and weigh the benefit to your career of accepting the assignment against the cost of decreased personal time. The point here is that a loss of personal time is never an automatic reason to say no to an assignment request.

Let's turn now to the last of the three difficult yes or no situations: deciding whether to accept an entirely new job or assignment in your organization. This may present the hardest of all yes or no decisions. Some of these requests clearly involve moving in a direction that will not advance your career. If you are in an investment bank and are asked to give up direct client contact to fill a staff position, you are being asked to get off the fast track and basically freeze your career. If you are at an investment management firm and are asked to stop making investment decisions and supervise the back office, that is likely where you will end your career. In your own organization you are likely to know the important but dead-end positions. If you are asked to take one of these, you basically have three choices: accept the position and start taking life a lot easier; try to persuade the requester that you are more valuable where you are; or start looking for a new job.

Sometimes, however, it is not at all clear whether a position change will enhance or kill your career. If it is not clear, ask a lot of questions, solicit the opinions of people you respect, search the Internet for information, examine the gender of the people in comparable or more senior positions, and take your time deciding.

Al: Caye is a friend at a large accounting firm. She had recently been promoted to manager when she was asked to accept a transfer out of auditing into the office of the firm's CFO. The move would mean giving up the chance to become a partner but it would also mean more predictable hours and greater job security. When we talked, I

(Continued)

tried to probe the depth of Caye's career ambitions. How important was partnership to her? Did she ultimately want to move from public accounting to industry? Did she think about careers outside the financial area, maybe even running a business herself? Caye was not sure of the answers to any of these questions, but she realized that if she said yes to the job in the firm's CFO's office, she would be cutting off all these other options. She was not willing to do that, so she said no. The firm was surprised but accepted her decision. As far as Caye knows, she is now on track to become a partner in another year or two.

One final word about deciding whether to say yes or no to a request that could affect your career: give yourself the time you need to consider the answer carefully—say, "Let me sleep on that, and I'll get back to you." One way to clarify your focus is to think about the advice you would give to a friend in the same situation.[4] Ask yourself whether the request is being made of you because you are a woman. How would a man in your situation respond? Exactly why were you asked to do this? What is the motivation of the person making the request? Do you think that person has your best interest in mind? Has anyone already turned down the request? What's likely to come next if you say yes? If you say no? Saying no to career-affecting requests is never easy, but sometimes saying no is the only way to keep your career on track.

APOLOGIES

What should you say or do when you have missed a deadline, screwed up a project, or upset an important customer or client? Men often follow the John Wayne maxim, "Never apologize, mister, it's a sign of weakness." Men are likely to view apologies as a diminution of their power and an increase in the power of the person to whom they give the apology. Because they see apologies as a power-shifting process, men will typically view a woman who apologizes profusely and dwells on her mistakes as weak and powerless.

Most women don't view apologies in terms of a power dynamic. If you are like most women, you probably view an apology as a way to repair damage to a personal relationship because of a serious mistake or lapse. There is nothing wrong with that view. Indeed, an appropriate apology can strengthen personal and professional bonds, ease conflicts and tensions, and make you more likable. The key here, however, is that the apology needs to be appropriate.

Here are some tips for deciding whether and what type of apology is appropriate:

1. You should be absolutely sure an apology is necessary. Not every mistake calls for an apology. Consider whether an apology is expected, whether it will reduce anger or disappointment, and whether it will promote a more harmonious relationship going forward. Unless you can answer yes to at least one of those questions, move on and put the mistake behind you.

2. If an apology is called for, you should make it promptly, forthrightly, and sincerely. Look the other person in the eyes, speak firmly, articulate your words without hesitating or mumbling, and be direct, sincere, and brief. Wait calmly for the other person's response, and as soon as the subject of your mistake has been addressed, move on to another topic without embarrassment or discomfort.

3. An apology is not an excuse. An apology is an acknowledgment of some failure on your part. It should not be an explanation of all the reasons why you made the mistake in the first place.

4. Be sure you apologize only to the right person. You don't need to tell your coworkers, "I am so sorry I bungled John's project." Apologize to John, put your head down, go back to work, and don't make the same mistake again. Emphasizing your mistakes by placing your regret on display makes you appear vulnerable, weak, incompetent, and lacking in confidence. A mistake is not a crime, and shame is not an appropriate emotional response.

5. Consider the position, gender, and personality of the person to whom you are apologizing. If you need to apologize to a senior man who has been unsupportive of your career aspirations, you need to think far more carefully about when, how, and where you apologize than when you apologize to a female coworker with whom you have a close personal relationship. Your apology in the first situation is likely to be far more important to your future career than your apology in the second. And, just because the situation is difficult, don't put off the apology or give it in an offhanded or half-hearted way.

EMOTION

A woman enters a minefield when she displays emotion in the office. Women are stereotypically assumed to be emotional but men are assumed to be unemotional. As a result, when a woman shows emotion, she is likely to confirm the gender stereotype of an irrational and out-of-control female.

A man arguing his position with passionate intensity is likely to be seen as deeply committed to what he believes in. A woman doing the same thing is likely to be seen as overwrought and excessively emotional. An angry man is likely to be seen as justifiably outraged or indignant; an angry women is likely to be seen as unprofessional or having lost it. And a man displaying his pride at a recent accomplishment is likely to be seen as competent and accomplished; a woman showing the same emotion is likely to be seen as a self-centered braggart.

To compete for career success in a traditionally male environment, you need to use attuned gender communication to show your feelings in ways that allow you to be seen as competent, intentional, and in control, not as irrational, excitable, or unstable. This imposes an unfair burden on you that your male colleagues don't have. But until the stereotype of the emotional woman goes away, it is something you need to keep in mind.

Crying

In our experience, there are six emotions that are particularly problematic for women in the workplace: anger, frustration, resentment, distress, sadness, and contempt. The first five of these—anger, frustration, resentment, distress, and sadness—are fraught with problems in their own right, but they are particularly dangerous emotions for a woman because they can trigger crying, and crying in the office is almost always a bad idea for a woman. Yet, a recent study found that over 40 percent of women (compared to less than 10 percent of men) reported that they had cried at work.[5]

There are biological reasons why women cry more than men do: women have a higher level of the stress hormone prolactin, which is associated with increased tears. Men have a higher level of testosterone, which reduces their tendency to cry. There are also social reasons: when a woman cries, it is seen as a reflection of her tender, caring nature, but a man who cries is likely to be seen as weak and lacking toughness.

Whatever reasons you might have in any given work situation to cry, we suggest you try to avoid doing so. Crying in response to work-related events—a lost customer, extraordinary pressure or stress, a poor performance review, a low bonus, or frustration with the way you are being treated—is likely to reflect poorly on your competence and leadership ability. Such a display of emotion implies that you are weak, unprofessional, and lacking in control and confidence.

Crying is also likely to embarrass other people, make them leery of criticizing you to your face, and invite benevolent sexism: "She needs care and should be handled with kid gloves." Crying over work-related events while you are at work sends the wrong message about who you are, what you are capable of, and what you want to achieve.

Telling you not to cry seems obvious but not particularly helpful. So we have found four techniques that can be effective if you think you are going to cry:

1. Rely on your sense of humor. If something brings you to the brink of tears, it probably has a humorous side: a quality of absurdity,

incongruity, bizarreness, or just plain silliness. Focus on this humorous side; as they say, it is always better to laugh than cry.

2. Change your location. Try not to cry in front of your colleagues; walk around the block, shut your office door, or go to the ladies' room.

3. Distract yourself. Try pinching yourself really hard, concentrating on a time you were particularly happy, or focusing on an entirely unrelated topic. In other words, shift your attention away from your current distress.

4. Imagine someone else in your situation. Think about the advice you would give another person about how she should behave in this situation. This creates an emotional distance from the problem, allowing you an opportunity to regroup, collect your thoughts, and find a positive way to deal with the situation.

Almost all work-related crying has a common core: a feeling of helplessness. Whether reacting to anger, frustration, disappointment, or resentment, women often cry because they feel they have no control over what is happening. It can be devastating to feel helpless in the face of hurtful, unfair, or unfortunate circumstances, and crying is an obvious reaction. But if helplessness causes you to cry, you need to gain control of your situation so you don't feel helpless. In other words, change the dynamics of your work relationships through more effective impression management.

One final comment about crying: crying at work is not the end of the world. Crying over a particularly disappointing, frustrating, or abusive situation is one thing, but having the reputation as an emotional crier is quite another. Figure out why you cried. Do everything you can to make sure it doesn't happen again. Find a way to gain a sense of control, and don't worry about people's reactions to your tears. Instead, concentrate on being seen going forward as competent, confident, and warm.

Anger

Anger is not an equal opportunity emotion in the workplace. Women and men experience anger with the same frequency and intensity, but for women, anger is probably the most dangerous emotion to display at work, apart from crying. A man can express anger without negative consequences ("He was provoked"), while a woman can seriously hurt her credibility ("She's out of control"). This difference in reactions to angry women and men is well illustrated by a 2008 study. Participants (110 women and 70 men) randomly viewed videos of job applicants. The applicants were professional actors (women and men) who performed one of two scripts: applying for a job and showing anger, or applying for a job and showing no emotion. Participants then rated the applicants as to their suitability for the job.

Angry female applicants received the lowest ratings, were offered the lowest salaries, and scored lowest in terms of competence (knowledge of their fields). Angry women were also viewed as more out of control than angry men. Notably, women participants were just as hard on angry women as were the men.[6]

Of course, a woman's status within her organization is highly relevant in determining the consequences she will face for showing her anger. An angry outburst by a female CEO is likely to be judged far differently than a similar outburst by an entry-level woman. Nevertheless, women leaders consistently report they must control their anger far more than do men. Women leaders report that showing anger will hurt their interpersonal relationships, a concern men don't seem to have.[7]

As unfair as it may be, you should avoid showing anger in the office. If you are angry and don't think you can control yourself, get away: walk around the block, have a cup of coffee, or call a friend. We are not saying that you cannot let others know you are angry, just that you should not do so in an emotional way: no yelling, screaming, ranting, or cursing. Express your anger deliberately, in a calm, forceful tone of voice. Strive to demonstrate your power, confidence, and seriousness. Look directly at the person with whom you are angry, explain why you are angry, and say what you expect to happen in the future. When you are justifiably angry and can control your anger without emotion,[8] you are in a position to make a very positive impression.

KEY TAKEAWAYS

■ **Speak with authority.** When you give out assignments, speak in a clear, direct, and unambiguous way. Explain what you expect to see when the answers come back to you.

■ **Learn to say no.** Try a simple "No, I can't help with that." If you are not in a position to say no, respond in a way that will allow you to successfully meet the request. Perhaps you can say, "I cannot deliver that project by tomorrow. But I can meet a Thursday deadline."

■ **Know when to talk.** When accepting an assignment, balance your need to ask questions with your need to appear competent, efficient, and a proactive problem solver.

■ Giving feedback or criticism is an art:
  - ➤ If the other person might not hear criticism buried in positive comments, drop the sugarcoating.
  - ➤ Focus on the event or problem, not on the other person.
  - ➤ Don't sacrifice your authority by helping a subordinate save face.
  - ➤ Don't forget that giving feedback to a supervisor involves political considerations.
  - ➤ If your feedback is met with aggression or belligerence, remain focused on making your points with clarity, neutrality, and temperance.

■ It's not personal. When you are getting feedback or criticism:
  - ➤ Don't take it personally, get emotional, or overreact.
  - ➤ Don't get defensive or make excuses.
  - ➤ Don't grovel.

➤ Don't leave the conversation without understanding what you need to do differently going forward.

■ A coping sense of humor is very helpful in many of these difficult and tricky situations you face in your career.

■ When saying no:

➤ Say no as infrequently as you can, consistent with your career aspirations. You want to have the reputation as a team player who is available to help out and accept new challenges. But after you have earned the right to say no, say it when necessary to keep your career on track.

➤ Say no graciously. Use attuned gender communication and use a pleasant yet firm tone of voice. Don't get cornered into giving an excuse for your unavailability other than that your schedule (or that of your team) will not accommodate another project. Express a sincere, "I'm sorry," but don't make it a lengthy apology. Focus on your desire to maintain the quality of your work and meet other requests.

➤ Take time to consider the request so the other person knows you have seriously considered it. Telling the requester you will think about whether you can accept the project can be a good approach, as long as you do not create a false expectation that you will actually accept the assignment.

➤ Let the requester know that you're involved in many other projects so it does not look like you cannot handle multiple projects.

➤ Put your boss's and your supervisors' requests ahead of requests from other colleagues who are asking for your help to meet their own responsibilities.

➤ Carefully evaluate the times that you say no so you are not viewed as avoiding or shirking your responsibilities.

➤ Keep in mind that saying no is often a give-and-take process and that the requester is likely to push you to change your mind. Be prepared to hold your ground.

- ➤ Explain, when appropriate, that by saying no you are protecting your team or meeting a schedule set by others. This allows you to show you are communal and likable because you are concerned about others.
- ➤ Offer to take responsibility for a piece of a project if you want to participate but don't have time to take on the entire project.
- ➤ Ask your supervisor to help you prioritize your projects so no one is disappointed by your project completion timing.
- ➤ Suggest other colleagues who might be better suited or have more time to handle the project.
- ➤ Be alert for compliments with a hidden agenda. If your boss tells you, "I can't imagine what we would do without your help," "You're the best," or "I can't thank you enough," beware. Is your boss softening you up to accept another noncore project?

■ When considering saying no:

- ➤ Don't say yes to projects that are irrelevant to your career advancement unless you believe that you don't have a choice.
- ➤ Don't be a doormat, good sport, or wimp who always pitches in if it compromises your ability to deliver required projects in a timely basis in the best form you can make them.
- ➤ Don't deliver a no by e-mail or through another person. Saying no in person (or on the phone if you can't do it in person) allows you to show appropriate respect.
- ➤ Don't say "maybe" or use uncertain words like "perhaps." Be direct and clear about your answer.
- ➤ Don't act as if you did something wrong by saying no. But be prepared for the requester to play on your guilt.
- ➤ Don't ignore the request, and don't pretend the other person never asked for your help. Check in later to see if the project was assigned. Show you actually care about the project and would have liked to help.
- ➤ Don't be evasive in your answers. You want the requester to respect your decision, not question your justifications.

➤ Don't say no because the assignment will be difficult or you don't want to work that hard. Revisit our grit discussion in chapter 4.

■ Use apologies appropriately. An apology should be given when you have made a mistake or are at fault for something. Don't forget that apologies at work are often part of the power dynamic between yourself and your colleagues.

■ Once you apologize, move on and give it up. Don't obsess about your mistake, don't keep bringing it up, and don't beat yourself up over it.

8

Meetings

Meetings provide you with some of the best opportunities to demonstrate your competence and leadership abilities. But many women find meetings problematic. In a 2014 *Harvard Business Review* survey of 270 female managers in Fortune 500 companies, more than half of the women reported that mixed-gender meetings posed significant problems or were a "work in progress."[1] Women tell us a variety of things about why they find meetings so difficult. They can't break into the discussions, and if they do, they are ignored, interrupted, or challenged; they get little airtime; their ideas are not acknowledged until they are repeated by someone else; if they speak with real conviction, they are criticized for being emotional; when challenged, they feel pushed out of their comfort zone; they become disconcerted or ill at ease if there is conflict; they believe the men talk, interrupt, and challenge too much; and they think men pay more attention to what other men say than to what women say.

Not surprisingly, men see meeting dynamics very differently. In that 2014 survey about meetings we just mentioned, more than a third of the male managers said their female colleagues fail to state a strong point of view, and fully half said that "women allow themselves to be interrupted, apologize repeatedly, and fail to back up opinions with evidence." The men frequently described women as defensive when challenged and prone "to panic or freeze if they lost the attention of the room."[2]

In the course of your career, there will be too many meetings attended by too many people with control over your compensation and advancement for you not to be at the top of your game when you are in one. Therefore, you need to be able to use meetings as occasions to network, display your unique perspectives, and showcase your abilities. In this chapter, we discuss practical techniques for doing just that. Meetings are likely to be the most frequent and, perhaps, the best opportunity you have to demonstrate your competence. Attuned gender communication will allow you to put a spotlight on your competence and warmth.

WHEN TO ARRIVE AND LEAVE

If your organization is similar to many with which we are familiar, women tend to arrive on time but men tend to arrive early, using the time before the meeting to catch up on business developments, test the waters about issues likely to come up at the meeting, joke with one another, or discuss sports or news events. If this is the pattern at your organization, you should arrive for a meeting in time for the "pre-meeting." Be relaxed, conversational, and interested in whatever topics are discussed. You want to be seen as one of the team.

You can use this pre-meeting to gather information about what people are thinking about and gain a sense of the interpersonal dynamics of the people who will be there: the leaders, the followers, the idea originators, and those with whom you are most likely to have difficulties. If you have an opportunity to discuss your thoughts, you should show your sense of humor and engage in vigorous give-and-take. But don't worry if you don't. Your primary purposes in being at the pre-meeting are to be seen as a member of the team and to gather information that will help you perform better when the meeting starts.

Just as there is likely to be a pre-meeting, there is likely to be a post-meeting wrap-up. You want to be a part of this wrap-up as well. Don't rush off when the meeting ends. If others stick around, you should too. This is a time to deal with conflicts and differences that may have come up during the meeting. It is also a time to foster alliances, learn how others feel about the decisions that were made, and strengthen your professional connections with the leaders and rising stars. Participating in such wrap-ups is an opportunity to build your network, show your interest in the organization, and make it clear that regardless of what happened at the meeting you have no hard feelings.

Andie: Juliet recently sought my advice about her apparently stalled career progress at a large pharmaceutical company. She had joined the company on the same day as Dustin. After only a few months, however, Dustin had a lot more friends than she did, and he was involved in more high-profile projects than she was. I suggested that she keep an eye on Dustin to get a sense of how he spent his day. Juliet and Dustin were in many of the same meetings, and Juliet realized that while she came on time and left promptly (so she could "get back to business"), Dustin arrived early and was one of the last people to leave. Juliet was puzzled. She didn't understand why her "greater efficiency" was not being recognized, or why Dustin was getting better projects when he was "wasting" all that time. At my suggestion, she started to arrive and leave meetings at about the same time Dustin did. Juliet was amazed at how much "business" was conducted pre- and post-meeting. Within a few months, Juliet was working on many of the same projects as Dustin. She told me she would never have believed how much more important pre- and post-meeting times were than her original concern for efficiency.

CHOOSE YOUR SEAT CAREFULLY

Leaders tend to sit at the end of the table or in a place where they can see all (or most) of the other attendees. Even if there isn't a pre-meeting, you should arrive early enough to pick the seat you want. Don't sit closest to the phone, the doors, the food, or the coffee—let someone else answer the phone, get the copies made, deal with the food, or make sure there is hot coffee. Wherever you sit, be sure you take up as much space as the men do, and resist the temptation to yield the space you have initially claimed. As you sit, hold your upper body erect and your lower body quiet. You should use body language that is powerful and expansive.

INTERRUPTIONS

Having a seat at the table is not the same as having a voice at the meeting. The number one complaint that women have about meetings is the frequency with which they are interrupted by men, and their complaint is in most cases entirely justified. Researchers at George Washington University, for example, asked pairs of women and men to discuss preselected topics for three minutes. On average in each of these conversations, women interrupted men just once, but men interrupted the women more than 2.5 times.[3] Moreover, researchers from the University of California at Santa Cruz found in a meta-analysis of forty-three published studies that the primary reason men interrupt women is to assert dominance in the conversation and take the floor away from them.[4]

The issue you face at mixed-gender meetings, therefore, is not whether you will be interrupted but how you will deal with the interruptions. You need to hold onto the floor, and it will be difficult to do this if you become intimidated, confused, or lose your confidence. But if you lose the floor, you not only lose the opportunity to present your ideas but will come off looking weak and lacking in leadership potential. So stand your ground. Don't be distracted or look uncertain or clueless. Don't let the interrupter bully you. You need to remain polite, calm, and pleasant, but firm and direct. Here are some attuned gender communication techniques for dealing with interruptions.

- Without raising your voice, in an even tone, look the interrupter directly in his eyes, and say something like, "Excuse me, John, I am not finished. The point I was about to make is..."
- If this is not the first occasion on which the person has interrupted you, you might say something stronger, such as, "Bob, I would appreciate you not interrupting me. You can speak when I am finished."
- If it is a very senior man whom you want to be careful not to offend or embarrass, you might try something like, "Rick, would you mind if I finished my point; it will only take a minute."

Whatever approach you use, you need to respond to an interruption immediately and then continue with what you were saying.

We fully appreciate how difficult this sort of direct, assertive response can be. The man may have stood up to speak, he may be considerably larger than you are, and his voice is probably louder and deeper than yours. Nevertheless, when you are interrupted by someone intent on taking the floor—rather than seeking a clarification or asking you a question—your confidence, determination, and leadership capacity are being tested in front of the other participants. With the right perspective on your abilities—the sort of perspective we discuss in chapter 4—you can develop the strength and determination, mixed with a good deal of pleasantness, to hold the floor when someone tries to take it away from you.

Dealing with a male interrupter may be particularly difficult because of gender stereotypes. When you assert yourself in an effort to hold the floor, you risk being seen as aggressive and unpleasant. If you give up the floor, however, you are likely to be seen as pleasant and likable, but not qualified for the competitive world of senior leadership. So here again is the familiar Goldilocks Dilemma: a woman is seen as too tough or too soft, but rarely just right. And, as in other double bind situations, the only way you can make the impression of being strong *and* likable is through the use of a mix of agentic and communal verbal and nonverbal behavior. In other words, you need to use attuned gender communication. When you tell John, Bob, or Rick that you are not giving up the floor, you should smile, use a pleasant tone of voice, and maintain an unemotional and nonconfrontational manner. But if pleasant is not working, it is better to be seen as competent and aggressive rather than likable and irrelevant.

There are a number of other ways to prevent interruptions from forcing you to give up the floor. Don't pause in a way that provides other people with the opportunity to interrupt you; don't use nonverbal behavior that appears to invite interruptions; keep your volume up; remain confident; ignore signals that someone wants to interrupt you; don't look at the people who want to interrupt you; and use nonverbal behavior to show your power (think power posing). There is some value in all of these techniques, but in our experience, when a man interrupts a woman to take the floor away from her, the only way she can effectively keep it is to deal with him directly, firmly, explicitly, and calmly.

Of course, in the best of all possible worlds, you would not have to deal with interrupters all by yourself. We have known and worked with several very senior leaders who, when chairing meetings, would not stand for floor-grabbing interruptions. In the absence of this sort of leader, however, think about doing the following:

1. Talk with key meeting participants before the meeting starts to share and discuss your ideas. Develop a strategy that allows you to make your points without interrupting one another.

2. If you are friendly with someone who will be at the meeting, agree to "protect" each other at the meeting. If either of you is interrupted in an attempt to grab the floor, the other should say something like "Let her finish," "I want to hear his idea," or "Wait your turn." Finding the right ally can make your meetings much more comfortable and successful.

3. When another woman is interrupted at a meeting, speak up for her. It is much harder for someone to take control of a discussion if he has two people to contend with, rather than just one.

These are just a few of the many techniques available to deal with interruptions, but ultimately there are only two rules to remember: don't let the floor be taken away from you, and hold on to it with strength, grace, and humor, the techniques of attuned gender communication.

IDEA THEFT

The classic Riana Duncan cartoon from *Punch* sums up the problem women have with their ideas being stolen.

The meeting leader tells Miss Triggs that she made an excellent

"That's an excellent suggestion, Miss Triggs. Perhaps one of the men here would like to make it."

Reproduced with permission of Punch Ltd., www.punch.co.uk © Punch Limited

suggestion. He then suggests that perhaps one of the men might like to make it so it can be taken seriously. It's wrong, it's not fair, but men (and often women) tend to pay more attention to what men say than to what women say. A woman can make a valid, interesting, or strategy-challenging point at a meeting and watch the conversation proceed as if she had not said a word. But, as in the Duncan cartoon, if her point is later restated by a man, the conversation is likely to take on a new focus, with the man praised for his insight and ingenuity. Once again, in the best of all possible worlds, when this happens, the meeting leader or another powerful person at the meeting should step in.

Al: Over the years, I have worked closely with Jason, the chair of a professional service firm, who is a stickler for recognizing idea origination. I was in one meeting when Wilma, a young associate at his firm, made a good point that was ignored until Rick made it a few minutes later. I still remember Jason looking directly at Rick and saying, "Thanks, Rick, for restating Wilma's point. I thought it was a good one too. Now, Wilma, do you have anything more to add?"

Unfortunately, such third-party intervention doesn't happen very often. You cannot depend on others to protect your ideas from theft. It is your responsibility to ensure you receive credit for your ideas. When someone attempts to steal your idea, you have a choice: you can claim ownership or remain silent. Either way has risks. Staying silent is safe in the short term, but it is the first step down a slippery slope away from career advancement. Claiming ownership of your contributions, however, risks hostility and criticism, but it also displays confidence and competence, two key traits that are necessary for career advancement. So once again, you need to use both your agentic and communal qualities to successfully achieve the "just right" of the Goldilocks Dilemma.

Another approach to claiming ownership of your idea is to use your coping sense of humor. Laugh and say in a light but even tone, "I am flattered that you thought my idea was so good it deserved to be repeated." Humor of this sort highlights your confidence without exposing you to criticism for not conforming to the traditional communal stereotype.

PILING ON

Once an idea has been accepted by key meeting participants, others are likely to rush to restate and reinforce the idea. This is commonly referred to as piling on. Unfortunately, it is rare for meeting participants to pile on to a woman's idea until it has been successfully stolen by a man. Therefore, you shouldn't expect that your ideas will be taken up, repeated over and over, and praised by your male colleagues. As a result, we encourage the women we work with to show as much support as possible for the good ideas presented by other women. When women openly support one another in mixed-gender meetings, it encourages all the meeting participants to recognize the value of the initial idea.

The second significantly gendered aspect of piling on is that because women are likely to be uncomfortable or see no point in piling on to an idea that has already been endorsed, they run the risk of being seen as not being on the team, or, worse, as contrarians, troublemakers, or pessimists. Be alert to when piling on begins. If you think the idea is sound but a distinction or clarification needs to be made, speak up and make it. If you agree with the idea, say you agree. And if you disagree, you need to make that known as well. If a consensus is being reached, you should let everyone know that you are firmly on board—or very much off the ship. This should be done pleasantly and in a nonconfrontational manner, but there should be no ambiguity as to where you stand on the ideas, actions, and plans that emerge from the meetings in which you participate.

Despite the value to an organization of encouraging and protecting dissenting views, if you dissent from the majority view, you can expect to be seen as uncooperative, unlikable, and having disrupted the harmony of the group.[6] You are also likely to face a backlash in the form of criticism, exclusion, and social and career penalties. You can avoid or minimize this backlash by dissenting in an articulate, thoughtful, and powerful way, but also projecting social sensitivity and concern for the good of the organization. Use inclusive speech techniques. Ask questions, assent to others' points where appropriate, use first-person-plural pronouns such as "we" and "our," and maintain a friendly and understanding demeanor.

VERBAL CHALLENGES

Men challenge women during meetings for one of two reasons: to assert power or to test the validity of their ideas and proposals. If you are challenged to justify a point you have just made—and the challenge is about the substance of your point rather than about asserting power—there is really only one way for you to respond: forcefully and articulately to defend your point. You don't back down, you don't say, "I'm not sure, but I think..." and you don't give up the floor by saying something like, "It wasn't very important." You have made a point that you thought was important enough to make, so you need to get into the rough and tumble to defend it.

AI: Kristen is a forensic accountant whom I have known for many years. She had recently finished supervising a huge project on which she had been working with a man she found extremely difficult to deal with. He would challenge her proposals and seemed to seek out occasions for confrontation. Kristen doubted he respected, much less liked, her.

A month or so after the project was completed, Kristen was attending a cocktail reception with her husband. This man was also there and he walked right up to them, shook their hands, and said to Kristen's husband, "Your wife is the most accomplished and impressive project team leader I have ever worked with." When Kristen told me about this incident, she said she realized immediately that their continuous verbal wrestling matches were his way of testing ideas, exploring possibilities, and verifying conclusions. Kristen told me she would never be comfortable using such a challenging, confrontational style but she gained a new understanding and respect for those who do use it, and she is now more prepared to effectively deal with them.

If your ideas are being challenged, collect your thoughts and explain in a firm, calm voice why your proposal makes sense: "The company is not ready for X because..." "Our division needs a new strategic direction because..." "That argument won't fly because..." You will never have a better opportunity to play a starring role at a meeting than in response to a verbal challenge. All eyes will be on you, and there is no danger that you won't be heard—unless, that is, you become confused, tentative, or uncertain. This sort of challenge gives you the opportunity to display your talents, confidence, and competitive spirit. While you should not be hostile or nasty, you don't need to try to be seen as pleasant and warm. After all, someone has just attacked your idea or proposal.

Verbal challenges that are not about the substance of your proposal, but rather represent an assertion of power, are not as easy to handle. There are two basic things not to do:

1. Don't become emotional. Passion is not your friend. Anger, sarcasm, and contempt undermine your credibility and alienate others.

2. Don't wilt or retreat; this challenge is about taking the floor away from you and nothing else. Any sign of weakness on your part, any sign you are soft, compromising, or defensive, will only encourage your challenger.

Power grabs in meetings are common and almost always directed against women or low-status men. Your most important ally in fending off such a challenge is your confidence. So before you go into a meeting, assume a power pose and mind prime as we discuss in chapter 4. Even though you are dealing with a hostile challenger who doesn't have your best interests at heart, he has given you an opportunity to demonstrate how tough, pleasant, and *prepared* you can be.

"AIRTIME"

Despite the stereotype that women talk too much, it is men who dominate mixed-gender discussions. A 2012 study found that men spoke 75 percent of the time at professional meetings even when women and men were present in equal numbers.[7] Women often find that at meetings they cannot get a word in edgewise, no matter what they do. But even in the most gender-biased organizations you can speak and be heard if you use the right communication techniques.

If you are not getting the airtime you want, figure out what *you* need to do differently. If you cannot get your points out, stand up, lean forward with your hands on the table, and say in a loud, firm voice, "I have an important point to make." If you are being interrupted, hold on to the floor. If you are being ignored, interrupt and repeat your point. Airtime is about who is regarded by the meeting participants as worthwhile listening to. You need to find a way to make the other meeting participants *want* to listen to you.

REACHING CONSENSUS

A typical meeting has as its objective the formulation of a recommendation or plan of action. Very often, women and men want to reach consensus in decidedly different ways. Women are likely to want to "think out loud" and explore the possibilities from all sides. The men, on the other hand, are likely to want to formulate a recommendation immediately, believing they have had sufficient opportunity to think through the problem.

The question is not which is the better approach, although we strongly suspect that the deliberative brainstorming approach produces the best result in most situations. Rather, the question is how *you* should behave if this sort of gender tug-of-war is going on about reaching a consensus. There are some obvious pitfalls you should avoid. If you try to keep the discussion open after the others have reached a consensus, they may think you are slow-witted, unfocused, or an obstructionist. On the other hand, you don't want to go along to get along. If you have a point that you believe needs to be considered before a final conclusion is reached, use the behavioral techniques we discuss in chapters 6 and 7 to make sure your point gets the attention it deserves. But be certain your point is important, not a quibble. Keep in mind that a group of businesspeople who need to make a recommendation must typically compromise. Be willing to move some distance to accommodate the views of the other participants—just not so far that you would not want to be associated with the recommendation.

Andie: Zineb is one of only three senior women (there are more than twenty senior men) in her department at a major multinational corporation. When she gets a new project, typically involving a technology innovation, she likes to think out loud with her team about different approaches to the project, exploring the relative costs and benefits of each approach and considering their different time frames and resource utilizations. Zineb recently came to me because she found that this approach made many of her male colleagues (both supervisors and peers) uncomfortable and impatient. After talking about the problem for a while, I suggested that before Zineb thinks out loud about a project or assignment, she should directly ask her colleagues if they would like to brainstorm with her or would rather reconvene after she formulates her plans. Zineb reported back to me that about

25 percent of the time her colleagues (almost all men) say they'd like to brainstorm with her; the rest of the time, they would rather pick up the discussion when she is ready to proceed forward. Although Zineb is no longer brainstorming with her team as much, she has much smoother interactions with them and finds it much easier to get buy-in for her ideas. They know they will have a chance for real input if they want it, but don't have to "waste" their time if they don't want to.

KEY TAKEAWAYS

■ Schedule enough time to attend not just the meeting but also the pre-meeting and the post-meeting wrap-up.

■ Stand up to be heard. If you find it difficult to get the attention you want, stand up. If you find that uncomfortable, use a use a chalkboard, whiteboard, or flip chart to have a reason to be on your feet. By claiming and holding your rightful share of physical space, you can play against, not into, common gender stereotypes, and appear more powerful.

■ Keep the floor. Consider the following ways to hold the floor:
  ➤ Increase your volume.
  ➤ Talk faster, but not too fast.
  ➤ When you pause to catch your breath, keep your gestures moving to fill the pause.
  ➤ Lightly touch the other person on the forearm to acknowledge you have more to say.
  ➤ You might also lightly pat the other person's arm to suggest he needs to wait a little longer.

■ Listen first. If you are challenged, always listen carefully to the question you are being asked and don't be afraid to ask to have it repeated so you understand it. If you are nervous or anxious, write the question down before responding.

■ Incorporate the question into your answer to help you stay focused. "You asked me how I got the number for the capital budget. Let me explain..."

■ Don't say, "I'm just thinking out loud, but..." This sounds weak and suggests that what follows has been poorly thought through, is tentative at best, and can be easily ignored.

■ Don't take verbal opposition personally. When you are the focus of such opposition, remind yourself that this is a linguistic style, not a personal attack. Don't back down; defend your ideas.

■ Jump in with both feet. Forget the concept of airtime. Don't wait for your turn to speak; it will never come. Come prepared and speak up toward the beginning of the meeting.

■ Put the notebook down. Don't volunteer to take meeting notes. If you are asked to do it, agree, but arrange with the meeting leader to have someone else take notes the next time.

■ Sticking to an agenda can prevent a contentious issue from derailing the central or important issues. Say something like "Time to get back to the agenda," "We've spent enough time on this topic," or "Next point."

■ In seeking a consensus, consider whether you should brainstorm. Others might not be comfortable with this and see it as a weakness.

9

Advocating for Yourself

The stereotype that a woman should be modest, unpretentious, and diffident creates another all-too-familiar Goldilocks Dilemma or double bind: if you conform to the modesty stereotype when your advancement depends on actively promoting yourself, your career will stall; if you forcefully advocate for yourself by highlighting your talents and achievements, you risk career and social backlash.

Two stories nicely illustrate this dilemma. The first is told by Rachel Simmons in her 2010 book, *The Curse of the Good Girl: Raising Authentic Girls with Courage and Confidence.*[1] A middle school English teacher at an elite all-girls school asked her students to write an essay describing their talents and best qualities. Her students rebelled. "They felt like they were bragging. They felt like they were being snobby. They felt like they were showing off." The teacher told her students that their papers would be private: no one would need to read her story aloud. They still refused. Her students were so distraught the teacher never did the exercise again.[2]

The other story is told by Joan C. Williams in a 2014 article in the *Harvard Business Review.*[3] Promotion at Google requires an employee to nominate herself or himself. When Google reviewed its promotion practices, it found that women were nominating themselves far less frequently than men. The women apparently believed that if they self-promoted and violated the modesty stereotype, they could adversely affect their career and personal relationships with other employees. Google began a campaign to signal to its women employees that self-promotion was expected; it hosted workshops on when and how to nominate oneself for promotion, and it included women among the workshop leaders. The gender difference in nominations at Google quickly disappeared.[4]

Several important points can be taken from these two stories. First, women generally don't like to talk or write about themselves in boastful, laudatory, or self-promoting ways. There may be many reasons for this, but one reason is surely that from early childhood, girls are told that it is not ladylike, if not downright unseemly, to explicitly call attention to their accomplishments. By age three, girls enforce social equality and avoid showing higher status by avoiding commands and boasts.[5] As a result, girls are far more likely to conceal their achievements and goals than are boys.[6] Because of this early conditioning, many women find self-promotion uncomfortable. They feel by doing so they are showing off, behaving in a conceited, unfeminine way.

Second, women learn very early that claiming social power or superiority triggers criticism by others.[7] When a woman calls attention to her talents, accomplishments, or ambitions, she risks backlash by being stigmatized, isolated, or penalized for violating the modesty stereotype.[8]

Third, when self-promotion is not only permitted but expected, as it is at Google, women feel safe to promote themselves and are entirely capable of doing it as effectively as men.

The modesty/self-promotion double bind is another instance of the familiar Goldilocks Dilemma of gender bias. If you are too modest, you cannot effectively compete, but if you assertively self-promote, you risk a negative backlash. Apart from this double bind, however, in situations in which you need to self-promote to obtain something of value in your career—a new job, promotion, salary increase, different work arrangement, or plum assignment—you are almost always competing for that reward against men, and the men have an inherent advantage over you in that competition.

Think back to chapter 1, where we first presented the basic female and male stereotypes. Women are assumed to be communal: affectionate, sensitive, warm, and concerned with helping others feel more at ease. Men are assumed to be agentic: aggressive, competent, independent, and leaders. Now, suppose a job recruiter is about to interview a woman and a man, both with MBAs from the same business school and comparable credentials. Let's imagine the thoughts that might be running through the recruiter's mind as he is about to meet the man: "He is confident, rational, independent, and competitive; his family responsibilities won't interfere with his job performance; he will fit in with our existing team; he won't raise any concerns because of his sensitivities; his accomplishments are due to his talents no affirmative action was involved in *his* achievements; he won't be needy or prone to emotional excesses; and he probably likes sports just as we do."

You can fill in the thoughts the recruiter is likely to have as he is about to meet the woman. Have we drawn too extreme a contrast? We don't think so. Before that female MBA candidate even meets the recruiter—before she can even attempt to navigate the modesty/self-promotion double bind—she is likely to have been judged a less attractive candidate than her male competitor. In other words, to use a sports metaphor, despite their comparable credentials, the man starts out a goal or two ahead of her—goals that *she* must score just to *even* the score.

This inherent male career advantage is just one more reason that women find advancing in traditionally male careers so difficult. Such advancement, however, is by no means impossible. As we have argued throughout this book, you can advance in your career despite gender bias. If you are able to use attuned gender communication to project both agentic and communal characteristics as appropriate, you will be able to deal with the modesty/self-promotion double bind and overcome the inherent male career advantage.

SELF-PROMOTION

Before turning to how to effectively advocate for yourself without risking a negative backlash, we want to say a word about how you should *not* self-promote. An alpha male's style of self-promotion is to blow his own horn loudly and frequently, unhesitatingly claim personal credit for team achievements, and routinely characterize his achievements, abilities, and potential as great, exceptional, and unique. When a man does this, he is conforming to traditional male stereotypes. He can ask for what he wants in an assertive, even challenging way and when he does so, he is likely to be recognized as hard-charging, with a good sense of his own self-worth. But in most situations, you are unlikely to get very far with this sort of behavior. You would not be conforming to but violating traditional gender stereotypes and would probably be seen—by both women and men—as pushy, conceited, and not a very nice person. This is an area where you simply cannot behave like a man and expect to be regarded as an effective advocate for yourself. In competing for career advancement, a woman who can be both agentic and communal can win, but a loud, aggressive, "in your face" woman has very little chance of doing so.[9]

Your most effective approach to self-promotion involves three pieces. First, you need to make a clear, strong, supported case for yourself. Second, you need to make this case in an inviting, pleasant, "I'm on your team" way so that you come across as competent *and* likable, confident *and* warm, competitive *and* friendly. And third, you need to score enough "goals" to even the score with your male competitors—and then score another one to win.

The hardest part of effective self-promotion is likely to be the first: clearly and forcefully presenting your talents and accomplishments. A recent study found that more than half of working women believe they are overlooked for promotions because they are too modest, too reluctant to be clear and direct about their qualifications, too concerned about being seen as arrogant, big-headed, or pushy.[10] Google eliminated this fear by giving its women executives "permission" to self-promote. You need to find a way to give yourself permission to stop worrying about appearing modest and, instead, persuasively present your talents and accomplishments.

Andie: I worked with Jean several years ago when she was up for a major promotion. She had been asked to prepare a memorandum detailing her qualifications for the new position. Jean was a dynamo when it came to promoting other women, but when it came to advocating for herself she felt uncomfortable, as she put it, "shamelessly talking about how good I am." Nevertheless, she wanted this promotion very much; she knew several men were angling for it, and she

(Continued)

realized that only one person was going to get it. She came to me to help her prepare her memorandum.

We worked on the memorandum for more than a week, gathering information and crafting an accurate but punchy recitation of her recent achievements. The memo discussed the new customers she had attracted, the success she had in building and strengthening her team, and an important policy initiative to which she had been a major contributor.

When the memorandum was finished, Jean wanted to show it to her office head before sending it to the committee that would make the final decision. She had not worked directly with this man and thought he would provide a good reality check. When Jean met with him, the first thing he said to her was, "Don't you think you should be more modest?" Jean told me this made her angry, but she stayed calm, smiled, and said, "I can support every word I have written." That was the end of the modesty discussion. After they had talked about a few specific points in her memorandum, he said, "I think you should go with this as is." She did, and she got the promotion.

I often think about Jean when I work with women who are trying to reconcile their modesty with their ambition. Women, in my experience, tend to be modest because other people tell them they should be. I tell them they can get by quite successfully with very little modesty, and if they display too much modesty, it will keep them from getting to where they want in their careers.

Your presentation of why you are fully qualified for the opportunity you are seeking needs to be forceful, direct, and attention holding. But it also needs to be nonconfrontational, engaging, and comfortable. In face-to-face situations, you need to maintain a pleasant facial expression, an even tone of voice, and a relaxed but erect body position inclined slightly toward the people you are addressing. Smile at appropriate times. When you claim credit for accomplishments, don't be afraid of using "I," but otherwise use inclusive language, including many instances of the pronoun "we." Avoid your higher voice registers, and don't appear angry, aggressive, or emotional. If you are advocating for yourself entirely in writing, as Jean was, have a good friend review it. Make sure it strikes the right balance between advocating for yourself and being a team player.

If your normal style of interacting with people is interested, caring, and engaged, you will do just fine with the being likable part of self-promotion. If this is not your normal style, study the earlier chapters on verbal and nonverbal communication, practice the exercises we suggest there, and don't give up. Every woman can learn to use both agentic and communal behavioral characteristics as she advocates for herself.

The last piece of effective self-promotion is dealing with the inherent advantage your male competitors have over you, scoring those goals by which you started out behind—and then scoring the winning one. If you are in a traditionally male career field, you are likely to be in an organization controlled by high-status, powerful men (and a few senior women) who constitute an in-group. Members of this in-group are comfortable with one another and with those coming up whom they view as like them. They are probably uncomfortable, however, with those coming up whom they view as unlike them, members of an out-group. This in-group/out-group dynamic is well illustrated by a 2010 study of the attitudes of senior executive men. It turned out that these men all used quite similar language to describe themselves, their most successful male employees, and their sons. In contrast, they had trouble making sense of or empathizing with their women employees' choices, goals, needs, and priorities.[11]

A particularly stark example of this in-group/out-group dynamic is provided by the entertainment industry. Recently, the American Civil Liberties Union (ACLU) of Southern California and the national ACLU Women's Rights Project asked state and federal agencies to investigate the "blatant and extreme gender inequality" in American feature films. Of the 250 top-grossing films in 2014, only seven were directed by women. As Jane Schoettle with the Toronto International Film Festival pointed out, filmmaking "is primarily about opportunities and if your opportunities are gated by those who don't give you the attention they might give to others *more like themselves*, you have difficulties."[12] Indeed, this situation is perfectly illustrated by Steven Spielberg's choice of a man, Colin Trevorrow, to direct the recent *Jurassic World*. Before *Jurassic World,* Trevorrow had only directed one half-million-dollar feature film, but Spielberg chose him because "he reminded me of myself when I was young."[13]

In your organization, the in-group/out-group dynamic may not be as extreme as it is in Hollywood, but in every traditionally male industry, profession, and job classification, there is a measure of suspicion and hostility toward those trying to break into the top ranks who are not like those already at the top. The people most subject to that suspicion are probably agentic women, women who are not like the women with whom these senior male executives are most comfortable: the noncareer women who are their wives and mothers.

When you advocate for yourself and ask for career advancement, you are challenging the status quo by asking members of the in-group to let a member of the out-group move up. To do this successfully, you need to pay careful attention to how you present yourself. Recall the eight-year study of business school graduates we discuss in chapter 3. The study found that women who used both communal and agentic communication techniques were far more successful in their careers—in terms of both compensation and promotion—than other women, whether solely communal or solely agentic, and all of the men.[14] Your ability to use both communal and agentic behavior is the key to your effectively advocating for yourself—and convincing the in-group you should be moved up.

Therefore, when you advocate for yourself, you need to forcefully and persuasively ask for what you want, but you need to do so in a warm, pleasant way that displays a genuine concern for the success of the organization and the people with whom you are dealing. The trick is to present your qualifications forcefully without coming off as an uppity, overly assertive woman who is unlikable and unlike the existing members of the in-group. By using the communication techniques we have been discussing in this book, you should be able to present yourself in such a way that you make an impression of competence *and* warmth, confidence *and* likability, and competitiveness *and* inclusiveness. By using both agentic and communal communication styles, you can neutralize your male competitors' advantage. Indeed, you can pull ahead of them and score the winning goal in the career advancement game.

One word of caution: if you are naturally a warm, pleasant, agreeable person, you are probably concerned about building and maintaining positive relationships with the people with whom you work. This is admirable and can be highly beneficial, particularly if you work on team projects. But it is important not to allow your desire for social harmony to lead you to settle for a less favorable outcome for yourself than you would have achieved if you had been less focused on personal relationships and more focused on getting what you want. You need to persuasively present your value and qualifications in a warm and pleasant way, but you should not let the negotiations end before they are really over. Being communal does not prevent you from also being agentic. In situations that require you to self-promote, you need to be both. And your objective in using both sorts of communication techniques is to advance your career, not to be the guardian of social harmony.

> *Al:* Jennifer is a friend who is one of the only senior women at a major financial institution. She encourages the women she mentors to speak and forcefully advocate for themselves when it comes time for a raise or promotion. She tells me she often gets responses like, "I know I should get the promotion rather than Bill (or Mike or Joe), but I hate his phony, self-serving behavior, and I'll be damned if I'll do the same thing." And Jennifer always responds to this sort of comment by saying, "So, are you telling me that when it comes time to put your kids through college and Bill has got the money from the promotion you deserved, you will be able to send him the tuition bills and he will pay them?"

WHEN TO SELF-PROMOTE

Self-promotion is appropriate in many situations in which you are not formally asked to present your qualifications. Linda Babcock, a prominent economics professor, tells the story of a group of women graduate students who came to her to complain that all of the plum teaching assistant assignments had been given to men. Babcock thought this was unfair and went to the dean to ask for an explanation. His answer was immediate and straightforward: "The men asked for the positions; none of the women did."[15] The female graduate students expected to be invited to apply. They assumed there would be a process for allocating teaching assistant positions, that all graduate students would be considered, and that assignments would be awarded based on the candidates' individual merits. The men didn't wait for such an invitation; they knew there were opportunities and went after them.[16]

The moral of Babcock's story should be obvious: career opportunities often become available without a formal invitation or selection process. You need to be on the lookout for these opportunities and quickly seize them. But even in situations in which there is a process, don't assume you can sit back and wait for the candidates to be evaluated on their merits.

Andie: A number of years ago I had lunch with Monique, a managing director at a major investment bank. I shared with her an early draft of my "Self-Evaluation Dos and Don'ts." After our lunch, Monique gave my draft to her boss, the partner in charge of the office. When he next saw Monique, he told her my observations helped him understand something that had long puzzled him. During the firm's annual promotion cycle, the men up for promotion always sought him out—some daily, others weekly, but all at least once—to tell him how great a year they had and why they deserved to be promoted. But the women candidates never reached out to him to make a pitch about why they should be promoted.

Hearing this, Monique mobilized her women colleagues who were up for promotion. She told them to each seek out the partner and tell him why they were qualified for promotion. Those women wanted to be promoted just as much as the men did, but they didn't think it was "appropriate" to lobby on their own behalf. They assumed that candidates for promotion would be selected based strictly on their accomplishments and that the people making the promotion decisions would have all of the information they needed—or wanted. Monique's encouragement gave these women permission to self-promote—and they did just that. Once the women understood that self-promotion was a necessary part of the promotion process, they did it as effectively as the men. Monique later told me it was a record year for women's promotions.

SELF-PROMOTION PREPARATION

You can think about the preparation for a situation in which you need to advocate for yourself as having two parts: content preparation and style preparation. Our suggestions will not be relevant in all self-promotion situations, but they are all worth keeping in mind.

Content Preparation

- Advocate for yourself with the same seriousness you would advocate for a client or your organization.
- Collect the information you need, develop a strategy, set your priorities, and prepare an outline that will allow you to present your qualifications in a compelling way.
- Present your request as a win for your organization as well as for you.
- Your request should be aligned with your organization's objectives.
- The justification for your request must be seen as accurate and complete.
- The justification for your request must be what your evaluators will be looking for.
- Demonstrate how your performance has met or exceeded your current responsibilities.
- Make your career objectives clear to your evaluators. They won't know what you want unless you tell them.
- Be prepared to respond effectively if you get pushback to your request.
- Anticipate likely questions and reactions to your request; prepare detailed responses.
- Keep a record of your achievements, compliments, recognitions, and awards, and use them effectively.
- If your evaluators do not know you well, the content of your presentation will need to be different from a presentation to people who are more familiar with you and your background.

- Managing the impressions others have of you is never more important than when you advocate for yourself.
- If possible, write out your presentation beforehand. Practice it with a friend and ask for a critique.

Style Preparation

- Watch how the successful and unsuccessful people in your organization interact with senior people. You can learn from both sorts of colleagues.
- Identify a presentation style that allows you to make your points forcefully but does not make you uncomfortable or feel "out of character." You need to come across as confident and accomplished. You can't do this if you are anxious, apprehensive, or ill at ease. There are many effective styles of self-promotion; make sure the one you choose allows you to come off as sure of yourself and your value, not as reluctant, shy, or frightened.
- Your presentation style needs to be appropriate for your objectives. What sort of impression do you need to make to demonstrate you are fully qualified for what you are asking for? If you want a new job or promotion, you need to act in a way that fits with that new role. If you want a raise, you need to present your achievements and their value to your organization. You also need to display the confidence and sense of accomplishment that comes from those achievements. If you want a challenging assignment, demonstrate the confidence, ambition, and skills to justify why you are qualified to receive what you are asking for.
- Don't forget to mind prime and power pose. And, if things don't go your way, rely on your coping sense of humor.
- When you make your presentation, think about your nonverbal behavior. You need to be engaging, persuasive, and pleasant.
- Prepare your written materials early enough so you can review, edit, and rewrite if necessary.
- Present your value in direct and positive ways. Use statements such as:

"This has been a year of phenomenal growth for me because of
_____."

"The projects I've handled have greatly increased my ability to do
the following _____."

"I have expanded my team's success in the following ways:
_____."

GETTING RECOMMENDATIONS

There are times when you will need to ask other people to advocate for you. These written and spoken recommendations are often critical to your career success. Unfortunately, the references women receive too often end up hurting, rather than helping them. Therefore, you need to pay careful attention to how you ask for references and what you tell the people who are going to give them for you.

The Problem

A number of recent studies have looked at the differences between the recommendation letters written for women and men. In a 2010 National Science Foundation study, researchers reviewed more than six hundred recommendation letters for approximately two hundred applicants who had applied for eight junior faculty positions at an American university. The researchers found that the reference letters for women typically used communal terms: helpful, kind, sympathetic, nurturing, tactful, agreeable, warm, and willing to help others. In contrast, men were typically described in agentic terms: assertive, ambitious, confident, daring, forceful, outspoken, independent, and intellectual. In addition, the recommendation letters for women often had ambiguous comments such as "she might make an excellent leader." But the letters for men were far more likely to have positive claims such as "he is an established leader."[17]

The researchers wanted to determine whether the differences between the recommendation letters for the women and the men affected the letters' value as advocacy pieces. To do this, the researchers removed the names of the candidates as well as all personal pronouns, and controlled for variables such as honors, the number of years the candidates had been in postdoctoral education, the number of papers they had published, the number of publications on which they had been lead authors, and the number of courses they had taught. The researchers then asked senior professors to evaluate the candidates based on these stripped-down recommendation letters. Their findings should hardly be a surprise—at least, not for the readers of this book. When selecting junior faculty, the communal traits so often used to praise the women candidates were hardly valued at all. Indeed, the more communal traits that were mentioned in a letter, the less qualified the candidate was judged to be for the position. And the more agentic traits a candidate was said to have, the more qualified the candidate was judged to be for the position.[18] Interestingly, men who wrote recommendation letters for women tended to use more agentic terms than women did when they wrote recommendation letters for women.[19] It appears that women think they are being nice to other women when they praise them in ways that identify the other women with traditional female stereotypes.

The devaluation of communal characteristics when it comes time to select people for positions calling for leadership ability is hardly limited to recommendation letters for academic positions. In a 2001 study of hiring behavior, researchers found that both female and male applicants with communal characteristics received low hiring ratings. But, as we have pointed out several times, female applicants who were able to exhibit both agentic and communal characteristics did not suffer a negative rating.[20]

In another study, researchers looked at more than one thousand letters for a position on the medical faculty at a large American medical school. Three hundred of these letters were written for women. The researchers found the letters for women were systematically different from those written for men. The women's letters were shorter, lacked basic features that the men's letters had, often raised doubts about the candidates' abilities (including negative language), and made explicit reference to their gender. The most common possessive phrases were "her teaching" and "his research," which reinforced the stereotypes that women are teachers and students, while men are researchers and professionals.[21]

What to Do

Whether you need a written or verbal recommendation, it will not be effective if it describes you in communal rather than agentic terms. Therefore, when you ask someone for a recommendation, discuss the kind of reference you need, your characteristics and achievements that are most relevant for the position, and the type of person the decision makers will be looking for. You need to help the people who will provide you with recommendations to formulate and present their recommendations.

KEY TAKEAWAYS

■ When you advocate for yourself, be prepared to answer all of the questions. Anticipate and prepare for negative reactions. When challenged, remain calm and confident, responding coherently and clearly.

■ Think about your potential. In seeking a promotion, focus on not just your strengths and successes, but also on your potential and the future advantages to your organization.

■ Don't be shy about your accomplishments. Don't downplay your own accomplishments by using terms like "we" or "team"—unless this is the only honest way to describe what happened.

■ Don't settle for less. You don't want to give up too soon. Make sure the conversation or meeting is really over before you stop explaining what you should get and what you are asking for.

■ Recommendations are important. You want a powerful recommendation that tells the reader important and relevant things about who you are and why you are suited for the position you are seeking. Don't ask someone for a recommendation unless you are confident it will be positive.

■ Inform your references. Always provide your references with information about the activities and projects that qualify you for the position you are seeking. Provide whatever other background information might be useful, so your references can provide you with the best possible recommendations.

10

Work and the Rest of Your Life

No matter how successful your career may be, unless you find it emotionally as well as financially satisfying, you are unlikely to believe the game is worth the candle. We have nothing useful to say about which career at which company in which industry or profession you are most likely to find personal satisfaction. But we do know that if you are liked by the people you work with, they will encourage and support you. When that happens, the chances are high your life at work will be enjoyable, worthwhile, and fulfilling, not just a way to earn a living.

But even a personally rewarding career is not the whole of your life. The rest of your life—your home, partner, children, recreational activities, and personal time—also needs to be satisfying and rewarding. The tricky part is achieving a challenging, stimulating, satisfying work life *and* a responsible, fun, deeply fulfilling personal and family life *at the same time.* Unfortunately, women are continually bombarded with two stereotypes about combining their personal and work lives that don't help them achieve satisfaction in either. "Work–life balance" and "having it all" are two gender stereotypes that often get in the way of women finding a sane, responsible, and fulfilling reconciliation of their careers and the rest of their lives. Let's examine these stereotypes and explore some more sensible ways to maximize the chances of finding that reconciliation.

WORK–LIFE BALANCE

Why do we call work–life balance a gender stereotype? Isn't finding such a balance a laudable objective for which we should all strive? Of course, but why then are only women told over and over again that they need to balance their career objectives with their domestic responsibilities? What about "balance" in men's lives? Given the current conversations about women and careers, it is as though a woman needs to find a cosmic balance scale on which to put her job on one side and the rest of her life on the other, that these parts of her life must be separate and unrelated to one another, static categories. Indeed, if every woman needs to find *the* balance of her career with the rest of her life, the components that make up her work and personal lives must be the same as they are for all other women, and there must be a single way that these components should be balanced that is just right for all working women. None of these implications of work–life balance is true. Work–life balance is a gender stereotype, pure and simple.

Having said this, we want to make it immediately clear that all people—women and men—need to find a satisfying reconciliation of their career and the rest of their lives. Such a reconciliation is absolutely essential to a successful, sustainable career as well as to valuable, fulfilling personal relationships. But there is no one way this should be done; different women will assign different priorities to different parts of their work and nonwork lives. Moreover, those priorities will inevitably change as a woman gains more career responsibility and acquires new personal responsibilities—a spouse or life partner, children, and aging parents.

We know many women who find their lives unsatisfying because they believe they have not achieved work–life balance. They feel frustrated and guilty as they cope with the inevitable tension between their careers and the rest of their lives. Indeed, many of these women are thinking about joining the 22 percent of women with professional degrees who are out of the workforce entirely.[1]

Men are often said not to have to struggle to balance career and family because they have wives at home to take care of their noncareer responsibilities: child care, meal preparation, housework, and all the other routine but essential tasks needed to maintain a semblance of order and comfort in one's life. Indeed, based on a 2014 survey of four thousand executives in a wide range of industries, 60 percent of the men have wives who don't work full time outside the home while only 10 percent of the female executives have husbands at home full time.[2] But in our view, this is just one more reason the career advancement playing field is tilted against women, and it is just one more disadvantage that you need to overcome to have a realistic chance of finding a satisfying and sustainable amalgam of your professional and personal lives.

This satisfying amalgam depends on choices you make with respect to a wide variety of things in your life: career field, size of organization, location, community, recreational and cultural opportunities, school system, and so forth. There are two fundamental, intimate issues, however, that are paramount in this regard: whom you choose to marry, if you decide to marry, and whether you choose to become a parent. These decisions and how you manage their consequences are the most important factors affecting your ability to find fulfillment both at work and in the rest of your life. We believe that seeking a work–life balance—as opposed to a fulfilling reconciliation—will not help you one whit in doing this. You can never "balance" work and life. You can only fit them together in more or less satisfying ways. If you start thinking about work/life choices, you are far more likely to achieve this sort of fulfillment than you are if you are focused on the need to balance these inherently interrelated parts of a whole existence.

Getting Married

If you decide to marry, the qualities your spouse possesses will be key to your achievement and maintenance of a successful, satisfying career–life amalgam. Apart from the obvious qualities of stability, affection, and compatibility, your spouse's support will be key to your career success. This support involves, at a minimum, two parts: fully sharing domestic responsibilities and sincerely encouraging your career advancement.

Many traditional men fail on both counts. With respect to domestic responsibilities:

- 37 percent of wives with successful careers help with their children's homework, while only 9 percent of men do.
- 51 percent of these wives take time off from work if a child is sick, but only 9 percent of men do.
- 45 percent of such wives clean the house, while only 9 percent of the husbands do.
- 50 percent of such wives prepare meals, but only 9 percent of the husbands do.
- 51 percent of such wives shop for groceries, while only 7 percent of the men do.
- 43 percent of these high-achieving women feel their husbands create more household work for them to do than their husbands contribute.[3]

The 2015 McKinsey study "Women in the Workplace" found that among women in entry-level executive positions, 44 percent report they do more home chores and 45 percent report they do more child care than their partner or spouse.[4] It is particularly at this entry level that women need to present themselves as fully committed to their careers; it is very hard to do this if your partner or spouse is not sharing equally in domestic duties.

You may be in love with a great guy, but if he thinks he can be on the golf course while you clean the house, you need to think very seriously about what you really want out of life before you marry him.

As for your potential spouse's encouragement of your career, many men's sense of their own self-worth and life satisfaction is closely tied to the traditional male stereotype of sole or primary breadwinner, financial decision maker, and guide and protector of the family.[5] How would your prospective husband handle your earning more money than he does? Working late? Traveling out of town frequently? Enjoying greater recognition and status than he does? These are not comfortable questions to think about, much less discuss. But if you are committed to your career and to being married, you need to know the answers to these questions before you tie the knot.

Perhaps most important, you need to know what your husband honestly expects will happen if there is a conflict between your career demands or opportunities and his. A recent survey of nearly twenty-five thousand Harvard Business School graduates found that 40 percent of the female MBAs reported their husbands' careers took priority over theirs and 70 percent of the male MBAs said their careers were more important than their wives' careers.[6] This perception of a decided difference in the career importance of women and men has a counterpart in the assumption of child-care responsibilities. A study led by an economist at the Federal Reserve Bank of New York found that the highest-earning female executives with small children spend twenty-five hours per week on child care, while comparably earning male executives spend only ten hours.[7]

Given the disparities in men's and women's attitudes toward work, home, and child care, it makes sense to learn before you marry what being married to *that* man will mean for your career. If you are already married and your husband does not fully share domestic responsibilities or is not an enthusiastic cheerleader for your career success, you don't need to give up on either your career or your marriage. We have watched many couples work through their conflicts over careers and domestic responsibilities with patient, extended conversations. In some cases, counseling was needed, but in all cases of which we have personal experience, the women are now doing great things in their careers, and their home lives. It is never too late to get it right, but accepting a grossly uneven division of responsibilities within your marriage or struggling to stay with your career when your husband wants you at home virtually assures feelings of resentment, hostility, and unhappiness.

Having Children

Even with the most supportive spouse or partner in the world, the decision to have children has major implications for both your career and the rest of your life. Obviously, the decision to have a child is a deeply personal one, and each woman brings different considerations to bear as she makes it. We know that for us, our lives are richer, fuller, and more enjoyable than they possibly could have been without our daughter. But being a mother brings with it career costs, new stereotype biases, increased domestic responsibilities, and increased expenses. It is not a decision to be made lightly—and it won't help you make a decision to think you have to find work–life balance.

The career costs of having a child can be high. A 2010 survey found that female and male MBA graduates earn similar incomes immediately following graduation, but ten and fifteen years after graduation, men's incomes substantially exceeded the women's. The researchers found this compensation difference to be due almost entirely to the career interruptions experienced by women with children. The study concluded that female MBAs with children had less accumulated job experience, more career interruptions, shorter work hours, and substantially lower earnings than both female MBAs without children and male MBAs with children.[8]

Perhaps because of the recognition of these career costs, millennial women with careers are delaying having children compared with earlier generations. For every year that a woman delays motherhood, her career earnings increase by 9 percent, work experience by 6 percent, and average wage rates by 3 percent.[9]

If you decide to have a child, regardless of the timing, you will face the maternal penalty we discussed in chapter 1. It is a disturbing but inescapable fact of life in the American workplace that women with children are viewed less positively than women without children.[10] While, at the same time, men with children are viewed more positively on the job than men without children.[11] And the maternal penalty does not stop there. The Harvard Business School survey of its MBA graduates found that among those women who left the workforce to care for their children, few did so by choice. Most of these women reported they had been pushed out of their careers by employers who stigmatized mothers.[12]

Mothers in the workplace can face a "death by a thousand cuts."[13] Why this hostility toward working mothers? In our view, much of this hostility is due to another gender stereotype: mothers cannot be fully committed to their careers because they are—or should be—fully committed to their children. Indeed, only 16 percent of American adults believe it is desirable for a mother to work full time.[14] Effectively dealing with the stereotype that you cannot be both a good worker and a good mother involves at least three pieces: your maternity leave, child care, and the allocation of domestic responsibilities.

First, pay careful attention to your preparation for and conduct during your maternity leave. Nearly 60 percent of women work full time during their pregnancy.[15] Eighty-two percent of women pregnant with their first child work to within one month of their due date, and many women continue to work right up to the time they go into labor.[16] A number of factors affect how close to your due date you decide to work: your doctor's advice, how you feel, the preparations that need to be made before your baby is born, and the help you have in getting ready for your baby. But apart from these obvious factors, your decision about your departure date sends a message about your commitment to your career. This varies from organization to organization, and we are not suggesting you work until you deliver your baby in the cab or Uber car that picks you up at your office. Our point is simply that you should be aware that everything you do once you become pregnant sends a signal about your career commitment. So take this into account as you decide when to start your leave.

Regardless of when you start your maternity leave, you want yours to be as smooth as possible with the least career disruption. Therefore, you need to prepare for your departure in such a way that you avoid three things. First, you don't want the projects you are working on to flounder or go off course. Second, you don't want to lose continuity, responsibility, or contact with your colleagues, clients, or customers. And third, you don't want to reinforce the stereotype that mothers are not committed to their careers. A few simple steps will help you successfully handle your maternity leave.

■ Let your colleagues know before you leave that you want to be kept up to date with what is happening with respect to your projects, position, and responsibilities; ask to be copied on important correspondence and e-mails; make sure that everyone has your contact information.

■ Develop a list of your active matters and projects, their current status, and their likely activity during your absence. Go over this list with your supervisors and discuss interim staffing needs. Talk with the people who will be handling your projects, make sure they understand the extent to which you want to be involved, and when and how you want to be contacted.

■ If you deal regularly with clients, customers, or suppliers, tell them of your pending leave and your expected return date. Make sure they know who will be handling your responsibilities during your leave and how they can reach you if they need to.

■ Periodically check on the status of your projects and relationships.

■ When you feel strong enough, an occasional visit to your office and periodic lunches with colleagues and superiors will help you stay connected.

■ Before you are scheduled to return from your leave, start to reconnect with your delegated projects and responsibilities. Find a way to involve yourself with projects and responsibilities that you would have handled if you had been at work.

■ Let clients, customers, vendors, and colleagues know when you will be back, and schedule face-to-face meetings with them to catch up on what they have been doing while you were on leave.

■ Don't come back to work until you are ready, but when you come back be sure you are really back. Work full days, if possible accept and seek out challenging projects travel if necessary and generally be available. You are now a mother who is also committed to her career.

Once you are back at work, you will need to be comfortable that your child is safe and receiving the attention and affection you want her to have. In our view, this means you must have an experienced nanny, a high-quality child-care facility nearby, a stay-at-home partner, or a fully dedicated relative or friend. We wish that high-quality, low-cost day care was readily available for everyone, but it isn't, and we don't see it coming anytime soon. High-quality child care and education are expensive. They are well worth the cost, and we don't think an ambitious, talented woman should ever end or cut back on her career simply because of that cost. But this is a complex, emotional, and highly personal decision that every mother must work through for herself.

As you pursue your career and take on the cost of high-quality child care, be careful not to fall into the trap of thinking that this cost should come out of *your* earnings, and that continuing *your* career after you have a child is a matter of *your* being able to earn enough money to justify the expense. Child care is a *family* expense and should be treated as such. If you or your partner think the cost of child care is your responsibility, that assumes your partner's career is more important than yours and that your career should continue only if it supports the additional costs of your being out of the house. This view inevitably leads to an unequal division of household responsibilities and a hierarchical domestic structure.

Apart from child care, if you and your partner are going to be working full time—the typical pattern for most married women with a career—there will also be all of those other domestic tasks—such as shopping, cooking, cleaning, laundry, bill paying, and home repairs—that the wives of the men with whom you are competing for career advancement are attending to. Andie often tells the women she advises, "You don't have to clean the toilets." But someone does. You will need a substantial support system if you are to stand a chance of successfully managing both your career and the rest of your life. Of course, if your partner shares equally with the domestic responsibilities, things will be easier, but even then, career success depends on having significant domestic support, which requires planning and additional expense. We believe that people who advise women about achieving career success without candidly calling their attention to the need for domestic help are ignoring the extensive support system a woman needs if she is to have both career success and a fulfilling life away from work.

Being a Mother While Pursuing a Career

Even with the best help in the world, many mothers have a deep feeling of guilt or selfishness when they are working and raising children, particularly very young children. This is often the result of the stereotype that mothers should be available to their children twenty-four hours a day, seven days a week. American culture is currently saturated with an ideology of intensive mothering, the belief that children's behavioral and emotional health and academic achievement depend on their mothers spending large amounts of time with them. It seems to be a common belief that the more time and attention mothers give to their children, the better adjusted and more successful their children will be. Indeed, a mother's time with her children is widely believed to be unique and irreplaceable.

In an important large-scale study published in April of 2015, however, researchers analyzed time diaries and survey data on approximately 4,400 families and close to 7,000 children in the University of Michigan's 1997 and 2002 nationally representative survey of families' activities and time usage.[17] The researchers examined three key dimensions of children's developmental outcomes: behavior problems, emotional problems, and academic achievement. They correlated these outcomes with the time mothers were engaged with their children and the time mothers were accessible to, but not directly interacting with their children. What the researchers found was that the amount of time mothers spent with children ages three to eleven and thirteen to eighteen, whether this time involved being directly engaged with their children or simply being available, had little effect on the outcomes of behavioral problems, emotional problems, or academic achievements. The researchers concluded there is no empirical support for the assertion that intensive parenting is beneficial for children. For adolescents, the researchers did find that a mother's engaged time with her children resulted in a "very small" effect on her children's delinquent behavior. But the researchers also found that a mother's time at work positively affected her adolescent children's math scores. In other words, mothers' work outside the home was correlated with higher math scores for their children.[18]

Apart from having no positive benefit, intensive parenting may actually harm children. Recent studies of college students show that those students whose parents have been excessively involved with their lives demonstrate less effective emotional coping mechanisms when compared with those students who have more hands-off parents. Excessive parenting can damage children's sense of autonomy and competence.[19]

As Julie Lythcott-Haims points out in her 2015 book, *How to Raise an Adult: Breaking Free of the Overparenting Trap,* college students with parents who had been intensely involved in helping them cope with day-to-day issues were not as open to new ideas and actions. In addition, college students with intensely involved parents were more vulnerable, anxious, and self-conscious than those students whose parents had been more hands-off.[20] Indeed, Lythcott-Haims, a former dean of freshmen at Stanford University, argues that overinvolved parenting—not giving children enough space to struggle through problems on their own— is taking a serious toll on the psychological well-being of college students. It is depriving students of the capacity for independent decision making.[21]

If you find yourself conflicted about being at work while your children are at home, keep in mind that no study has ever found that a mother's work outside her home had an adverse effect on a child's well-being. Indeed, as Kathleen McGinn, a professor at Harvard Business School, recently found, a mother's working outside the home may provide her children with positive benefits. McGinn found that women whose mothers worked outside the home are more likely to have jobs themselves, hold supervisory responsibility at those jobs, and earn higher wages (23 percent more) than women whose mothers had stayed home full time.[22] And being a working mother does not hurt men either. Men raised by working mothers are no less likely to have successful careers than other men, and they are more likely to share household tasks and spend more time caring for other family members. McGinn, commenting on her research, writes that there is "a lot of parental guilt about having both parents working outside the home. But what this research says to us is that [by doing so] you're . . . helping your kids."[23]

"HAVING IT ALL"

"Having it all" is another stereotype that is held out as a goal for women with respect to their careers and their families—but never (except with irony or humor) as a goal for men. The phrase is now brought out in virtually every debate over whether women can have full-time careers while responsibly raising their children. But in contrast to the generally upbeat attitude in the 1970s and '80s, when it was typically assumed that talented, ambitious women would be able to have it all, the prevailing attitude has recently turned sour and starkly negative. PepsiCo CEO Indra Nooyi, speaking at the Aspen Ideas Festival in 2014, said, "I don't think women can have it all. I just don't think so."[24] Christine Lagarde, head of the International Monetary Fund, in an interview with NBC in 2012 said, "I think you cannot have it all at the same time."[25] And in February of 2015, Drew Barrymore said in *More* magazine, "Women can't do it all."[26]

What does "having it all" mean anyway? Obviously it is not meant to be taken literally, say, having a home in the Hamptons, a penthouse overlooking Central Park, and children who are world-class athletes and Nobel Prize–winning scientists. But even if we understand having it all in a more limited way—say, to mean that a woman has both a successful career and healthy, happy, intelligent, well-adjusted children—would that really be "having it all"? For a woman to truly have it all, wouldn't she also need adequate personal time, a fulfilling marriage or personal relationship, close family and friends, a healthy lifestyle with sufficient exercise, educational travel, adventuresome reading, civic engagement, spiritual reflection, enjoyable hobbies, community participation, opportunity for aesthetic enjoyment, and so on?

But, of course, if this is what having it all means, the very notion is absurd. No one can have it all; everyone has to pick and choose what she (or he) wants to have and what she wants to do. So the right question is not whether women can have it all, but whether they can have what they sensibly want to have—and whether they can sensibly want a highly successful career and to raise well-adjusted, happy, and successful children. We believe the answer to *that* question is a resounding yes.

Perhaps the best-known recent discussion of why women can't have it all is Anne-Marie Slaughter's 2012 article in the *Atlantic* entitled, "Why Women Still Can't Have It All."[27] By having it all, Slaughter means something that on its face appears to be quite modest: holding a high-level job and having the time and capacity to deal with the needs of her children. She argues vigorously, however, that a woman cannot do both—that is, unless, in her words, the woman is a "superwoman." Slaughter does not state explicitly why a man can have both a career and children while a woman can't, but she provides hints. Her basic premise is that women have to make compromises when they combine a career and a family—compromises that men are far less likely to have to make. The reason for this, Slaughter tells us, is that women do not "*feel* as comfortable as men do" (her emphasis) leaving much of the care of their children with someone else, even their partners. Men "seem more likely to choose their job at a cost to their family, while women seem more likely to choose their family at a cost to their job." This difference between women and men is the result, in Slaughter's view, of "a maternal imperative felt so deeply that the 'choice' is reflexive."[28]

A woman's maternal imperative is a topic about which we have no interest in venturing an opinion. Whether such an imperative exists; if so, whether it is due to nature or nurture; whether it is felt by all women to the same degree; and how some women manage to perform well at both high-stakes jobs and child rearing are questions fraught with far too intensely felt political and social values for us to be foolish enough to comment. With that said, we have two general comments about the points Slaughter raises.

First, we believe that the claim that women must choose their career at the cost of their children or their children at the cost of their career is for most women simply a false choice. In Slaughter's case, she was a very high-ranking official in the U.S. State Department with a teenage son who was having problems at school and had hardly spoken to her for months. She was living five days a week in a city away from her family, working extremely long hours with no time for personal matters, and with a four-and-a-half-hour trip to go from her home to her job and then another four-and-a-half hours to get home again. Deciding that with *that* job a woman could not also responsibly raise a troubled child is hardly a valid basis for concluding that women cannot hold high-pressure, high-status jobs while raising children. We would never suggest that having a demanding career and raising well-adjusted children is a piece of cake, but unless you are in a situation—as Slaughter was—in which only genuine superwomen can do both, managing a career and a family is entirely possible even for mere mortal women.

Second, Slaughter proposes a series of workplace reforms: change the culture of face time, revalue family values, redefine the arc of a successful career, rediscover the pursuit of happiness, and enlist men. She writes nothing, however, about how these reforms are going to come about, other than speculating that more women in leadership positions could make it easier for other women to stay in the workplace. Slaughter is completely silent, however, about what mothers with careers can do now, before such reforms are implemented. Ultimately, we believe Slaughter's message is one of resignation, diminished ambitions, and frustration. We refuse to buy what she is selling.

Recognizing that you can have everything you sensibly want to have does not mean, however, that you can sensibly want everything. If you want to have a high-powered career and children, go for it. But this will mean you may have to give up some of your other aspirations, such as nonbusiness travel, training for a marathon, civic committees, university extension courses, a book project, or something else. If you want a serious career and to be a mother, these two pursuits—together with a fulfilling relationship with your partner—need to be treated as the most important things in your life. That means when something else conflicts with your career or your family, that something else needs to be moved aside. This is not as hard as it may sound. You prioritize now at your job; you simply need to start prioritizing your life as a whole. When career, children, and a partner are the things that matter most to you, everything else is relegated to a subsidiary role.

KEY TAKEAWAYS

■ Don't try to balance work and the rest of your life. They play different roles throughout your life. Choose what you value most in your life and prioritize your responsibilities accordingly.

■ Choosing a life partner is a decision that will have a profound and long-lasting impact on your career. Consider whether this person will value your professional ambitions and support you as you advance.

■ Prepare for maternity leave by meeting with your supervisors and advising them of how you have planned for your work duties to be handled in your absence.

■ During maternity leave, understand the status of your projects at work. When your maternity leave is close to ending, schedule face-to-face meetings with colleagues and supervisors to help you get up to speed before actually returning.

■ When you return to work, be fully engaged. You are now fighting against negative stereotypes about working mothers. Prove your value and your commitment to your career by volunteering for challenging projects, making yourself visible when you are in the office, and accepting travel assignments.

■ Don't feel guilty for enjoying your career and working full time. As studies have demonstrated, children are not harmed when their mothers work full time. In fact, your career may actually be helping your children become more self-sufficient and confident, with more egalitarian views.

■ Understand that you can have whatever you sensibly want, but there are costs associated with every dream.

CONCLUSION

This book is an extended argument about how women can achieve career success and why most of what they have been told about how to do this is wrong or unhelpful. The world of work, particularly the world of work in traditionally male career fields, saw dramatic changes from the middle 1960s to the middle 1990s. Since then, however, there have been few changes, and women's overall career achievements seem stalled. Women are beginning in virtually all high-status, high-paying careers in numbers comparable to men (engineering and information technology are conspicuous exceptions), but women are not advancing in those careers at the same pace or to the same extent as men. Because of their lack of progress, women are told a number of things. They are told they need to fix themselves: change the way they talk; act more like men; become more ambitious; ask for what they want; delay having children; and learn to be better negotiators. At the same time, they are being told that they don't need to fix themselves and that workplaces are what needs to be fixed: the demand for extensive face time needs to be ended; more flexibility should be provided; longer maternity leaves should be mandated; reentry training should be offered; quality child care should be provided at little or no cost; telecommuting should be an option; and stricter laws should be passed to assure equal pay for equal work. And, finally, women are told that unless their workplaces are fixed, they will never be able to have a successful career and a satisfying family life: they can't have it all or, at least, not all at the same time.

As we hope we have made clear, women don't need to be fixed; our workplaces (as much as they need fixing) are not likely to be fixed within a time frame meaningful to women in their careers today; and despite the practices and policies of the American workplace, women can have it all and have it all at the same time, if that means having a high-powered career, a loving, fulfilling relationship with a partner or spouse, and healthy, well-adjusted, successful children.

It is not women's fault that they have achieved less career success than men. The fault lies with the gender biases operating within all business and professional organizations. Because of these biases, women must compete for career advancement on a playing field that is severely tilted against them. This book is in one sense highly pessimistic because we do not see this career playing field becoming significantly fairer anytime soon. But in another, far more important sense, this is an extremely optimistic book. We believe women have the ability—right now and just as they are—to move forward in their careers in a manner comparable to men despite the tilt of the field.

To do this, women must recognize that the gender stereotypes held by their career gatekeepers are the primary obstacles to their career success, and they must learn to use communication techniques that will enable them to avoid or overcome these obstacles. The problem is not women's ambition, power, or competence but the pervasiveness and strength of these hurtful gender stereotypes and the unavailability until now of a systemic program for combatting these stereotypes.

This book is that program. It presents an integrated series of steps, what we call attuned gender communication, that you can use as you pursue your career goals. With attuned gender communication, we believe you, as a talented, ambitious woman, can successfully pursue your career without gender bias sapping your ambition or delaying or destroying your career opportunities. Attuned gender communication doesn't guarantee you career success, but it does guarantee your career won't stall or derail simply because you are a woman.

Based on the workshops we have run and the coaching we have done, we expect that there will be parts of this book that you will want to read more than once. And, indeed, if there are points about which you would like more information, we hope you will contact us at our website, AndieandAl.com. We would also like to hear about your experiences in using attuned gender communication. We very much hope that we've provided you with the techniques to realize your career dreams. Be sure to let us know how you think we can make our advice even more helpful.

One final word: a successful, challenging, satisfying career is within your reach. Go for it!

ACKNOWLEDGMENTS

The time, effort, and ideas of many people have gone into the writing of this book. Starr M. Rayford has provided us with editorial and research support that has helped us sharpen our prose, organize the manuscript, and coordinate its completion. Kay Bowers has been tirelessly good humored as she typed and retyped our many drafts and revisions. Kristine Johnson, Katie Ahern, Margaret Hanson, Olivia Clark Silver, and Dan Lambert have read and reread draft chapters, always providing insightful, constructive comments. At the risk of missing some of our reviewers, commenters, supporters, and others, we would like to thank the following: Bethany Harris, Ann Fourt, Darla Zink, Charlie and Rochelle Curtis, Mary Jo Stockman, Angela Corsa, Elizabeth Kroger, Judy and Adrian Coté, Brenda Dunn-Kinny, Wendy Manning, Jessica Cullen Smith, Wendy White-Eagle, Leslie Fenton, Rose Stubi, Steve Pflaum, Ruth Goran, Jennifer Mikulina, Krista Vink-Venegas, Angela Vasandani, Lee Richard Tschanz, Melinda Kleehamer, Mary Pat Farrell, Jen Berman, Wileen Chick, Marc S. Zaslavsky, Frances H. Krasnow, Susan J. Schmitt, Marlene Greenberg, The Dancin' Queens, Jennifer Wojan, Candace P. Davis, Cheryl S. Wilson, Jill Melnicki, Mary Wuilloud, Emily Vasiliou, Carol Frohlinger, Mary Lou Pier, Pam Simon, Robin Hadrick, Robin Cantor, Suzanne DeVries, Vickie Drendel, Ellen Turner, Kinga Staromiejska, Yang Connita Yang, Erica Harris, Catherine and Michael Zuckert, Valencia Ray, Tina Davis Milligan, and Kathleen Callahan.

We would also like to thank everyone at our publisher, Bibliomotion, for their first-rate professionalism and advice, with a special shout-out going to Alicia Simons, Erika Heilman, and Jill Friedlander. Also thanks to Lee McEnany Caraher who suggested we work with Bibliomotion in the first place.

We would like to provide a heartfelt thanks to Ursula Laskowski and Gloria Thomas for the extra work they willingly assumed to keep us organized, focused, and well provided for. And to Robin Ruesch for keeping things moving in the right direction for Andie at McDermott.

And we would like to end with a huge thanks to everyone who shared their stories and situations with us. Some of you will see yourselves in our anecdotes, but as we promised, we have changed your names and other career-related characteristics that might otherwise identify you.

NOTES

Andie's Preface

1. "The Equality Equation: 5 Ways Women Can Confront—and Rise Above—Gender Stereotypes," *Insight*, Summer 2015, icpas.org/insight.htm; "Developing Clout While Navigating Gender Bias," NAWL's *Women Lawyers Journal* 100(3), (Summer 2015); "Taking Control: Women, Gender Stereotypes and Impression Management," with Alton B. Harris in *Women's Bar Association of Illinois Newsletter,* Winter 2014; *What You Need to Know About Negotiating Compensation*, with Carol Frohlinger and Jane DiRenzo Piggott, American Bar Association Presidential Task Force on Gender Equality and the Commission on Women in the Profession, June 18, 2013; "Professional Advancement and Gender Stereotypes: The 'Rules' for Better Gender Communications," *Women's Bar Association of Illinois Newsletter,* Fall 2011; "Self-Evaluations: Dos and Don'ts," *Women's Bar Association of Illinois Newsletter,* Fall 2011; "Additional Things Women Can Do for Themselves," *Women's Bar Association of Illinois Newsletter,* Fall 2011; "What Professional Organizations Should Do to Advance Their Women Leaders," *Women's Bar Association of Illinois Newsletter,* Fall 2011; "The Design, Development and Implementation of a Women's Initiative," with Lisa B. Horowitz, Sharon Meit Abrahams, and Susan Smith Ross, Case Study 4 in "Implementing Women's Initiatives in the Modern Law Firm," *Managing Partner Magazine*, October 2007; "Bragging Rights: Self-Evaluation Dos and Don'ts," NAWL's *Women Lawyers Journal,* Summer 2007.

Introduction

1. Rachel Thomas, "Corporate America Is Not on the Path to Gender Equality," Lean In, September 30, 2015, accessed October 4, 2015, http://leanin.org/news-inspiration/corporate-america-is-not-on-the-path-to-gender-equality/; McKinsey & Company, "Women in the Workplace," McKinsey & Company Insights & Publications, September 2015, accessed October 4, 2015, http://www.mckinsey.com/insights/organization/women_in_the_workplace.

2. Judith Warner, "The Women's Leadership Gap: Women's Leadership by the Numbers," Center for American Progress, August 4, 2015, accessed September 19, 2015, https://www.americanprogress.org/issues/women/report/2015/08/04/118743/the-womens-leadership-gap/.

3. Catalyst, "Women CEOs of the S&P 500," April 3, 2015, accessed September 19, 2015, http://www.catalyst.org/knowledge/women-ceos-sp-500; Warner, "The Women's Leadership Gap."

4. Warner, "The Women's Leadership Gap."

5. Warner, "The Women's Leadership Gap."

6. Warner, "The Women's Leadership Gap."

7. Warner, "The Women's Leadership Gap."

8. Warner, "The Women's Leadership Gap."

9. Deborah Rhode's 2014 book *What Women Want: An Agenda for the Women's Movement* provides an excellent discussion of needed legal and organizational changes. She lays out a persuasive case for specific legal and institutional changes that would positively affect women's career success. With respect to legal reform, Rhode suggests enactment of the Paycheck Fairness Act, mandated equal pay for equivalent jobs, changes in the standards of proof in sexual discrimination cases, and required employer disclosure of relevant information about gender differences in promotions, compensation, and mentoring. With respect to workplace initiatives, Rhode suggests centralized organizational responsibility to develop and oversee gender equity initiatives, rewards for successful diversity initiatives, and a requirement that recruiters objectively justify their personnel decisions. And, with respect to work and family policies, Rhode suggests paid family leave, universal child care, prekindergarten education, legal protection against pregnancy discrimination, guaranteed six-week partial pay for serious health issues or child care, and enactment of both the Comprehensive Child Development Act and the Flexibility for Working Families Act. Deborah Rhode, *What Women Want: An Agenda for the Women's Movement* (Oxford: Oxford University Press, 2014).

10. Cecilia E. Ford, *Women Speaking Up: Getting and Using Turns in Workplace Meetings* (London: Palgrave Macmillan, 2008) (emphasis in the original).

11. David Hume, "Of the Standard of Taste," *The Philosophical Works of David Hume: Including All Essays and Exhibiting the More Important Alterations and Corrections in the Successive Editions Published by the Author,* in four volumes, vol. 3 (Boston: Little, Brown and Company, 1909–14).

12. Jeanine Prime and Corinne A. Moss-Rasusin, "Engaging Men in Gender Initiatives: What Change Agents Need to Know," Catalyst, May 4, 2009, accessed September 19, 2015, http://www.catalyst.org/knowledge/engaging-men-gender-initiatives-what-change-agents-need-know.

Chapter 1

1. Mahzarin Banaji and Anthony Greenwald, *Blindspot: Hidden Biases of Good People* (New York: Delacorte Press, 2013).
2. Sreedhari D. Desai, Dolly Chugh, and Arthur P. Brief, "The Organizational Implications of a Traditional Marriage: Can a Domestic Traditionalist by Night be an Organizational Egalitarian by Day?," UNC Kenan-Flagler Research Paper No. 201319, accessed April 18, 2015, http://papers.ssrn.com/sol3/papers.cfm?abstract_id=2018259##.
3. Sandra Lipsitz Bem, "The Measurement of Psychological Androgyny," *Journal of Consulting and Clinical Psychology* 42 (1981): 155–162.
4. David Schweider, *The Psychology of Stereotyping* (New York: The Guilford Press, 2004).
5. We use the term "agentic" in this book because we believe it is better to refer to these traits as agentic, rather than as masculine. Both women and men have these traits.
6. We use the term "communal" in this book because we believe it is better to refer to these traits as communal rather than feminine. Both women and men have these traits.
7. Carol T. Kulik and Mana Olekalns, "Negotiating the Gender Divide: Lessons from the Negotiation and Organizational Behavior Literatures," *Journal of Management* 38(4) (2012): 1387–1415.
8. Corinne A. Moss-Rascusin, John F. Dovidio, Victoria L. Brescoll, Mark J. Graham, and Jo Handelsman, "Science Faculty's Subtle Gender Biases Favor Male Students," *PNAS* 109(41) (2012): 16474–16479.
9. Moss-Rascusin et al., "Science Faculty's Subtle Gender Biases Favor Male Students."
10. Mark D. Agars, "Reconsidering the Impact of Gender Stereotypes on the Advancement of Women in Organizations," *Psychology of Women Quarterly* 28(2) (2004): 103–111.
11. Catalyst, "Women 'Take Care,' Men 'Take Charge': Stereotyping of U.S. Business Leaders Exposed," accessed April 18, 2015, http://www.catalyst.org/knowledge/women-take-care-men-take-charge-stereotyping-us-business-leaders-exposed.
12. Catalyst, "Women 'Take Care,' Men 'Take Charge.'"
13. Pershing LLC, "Americans Crave a New Kind of Leader—and Women Are Ready to Deliver," February 25, 2014, accessed April 18, 2015, https://www.pershing.com/our-thinking/thought-leadership/americans-crave-a-new-kind-of-leader-and-women-are-ready-to-deliver.
14. Pershing LLC, "Americans Crave a New Kind of Leader."
15. Pershing LLC, "Americans Crave a New Kind of Leader."
16. Pershing LLC, "Americans Crave a New Kind of Leader."
17. Pershing LLC, "Americans Crave a New Kind of Leader."

18. Benoit Dardenne, Muriel Dumont, and Thierry Bonier, "Insidious Dangers of Benevolent Sexism: Consequences for Women's Performance," *Journal of Personality and Social Psychology* 93(5) (2007): 764–779.

19. Monica Biernat, M. J. Tocci, and Joan C. Williams, "The Language of Performance Evaluations: Gender-Based Shifts in Content and Consistency of Judgment," *Social Psychology and Personality Science* 3(2) (2012): 186–192.

20. Eden B. King, Whitney Botsford, Michelle R. Hebl, Stephanie Kazama, Jeremy F. Dawson, and Andrew Perkins, "Benevolent Sexism at Work: General Differences in the Distribution of Challenging Developmental Experiences," *Journal of Management* 38(6) (2012): 1842.

21. Irene E. De Pater, Annelies E. M. Van Vianen, Agneta H. Fischer, and Wendy P. Van Ginkel, "Challenging Experiences: Gender Differences on Task Choice," *Journal of Managerial Psychology* 24(1) (2009): 4–28.

22. Laurie A. Rudman and Peter Glick, "Feminized Management and Backlash Towards Agentic Women: The Hidden Costs to Women of a Kinder, Gentler Image of Middle Managers," *Journal of Personality and Social Psychology*, 77(5) (1999): 1004–1010.

23. Deborah A. Prentice and Erica Carranza, "What Women and Men Should Be, Shouldn't Be, Are Allowed to Be, and Don't Have to Be: The Contents of Prescriptive Gender Stereotypes," *Psychology of Women Quarterly* 26 (2002): 279–280.

24. Kulik and Olekalns, "Negotiating the Gender Divide: Lessons from the Negotiation and Organizational Behavior Literatures."

25. Andrea Kupfer Schneider, Catherine H. Tinsley, Sandra Cheldelin, and Emily T. Amanatullah, "Likeability vs. Competence: The Impossible Choice Faced by Female Politicians, Attenuated by Lawyers," *Duke Journal of Gender Law and Policy* 17 (2010): 363–384.

26. "As Academic Gender Gap Declines, There Is Still Work to be Done," *Harbus*, April 25, 2011, accessed April 18, 2015, http://www.harbus.org/2011/gender-gap/.

27. Jodi Kantor, "Harvard Business School Case Study: Gender Equity," *New York Times*, September 7, 2013, accessed April 18, 2015, http://www.nytimes.com/2013/09/08/education/harvard-case-study-gender-equity.html.

28. Stephen Benard and Shelley J. Correll, "Normative Discrimination and the Motherhood Penalty," *Gender and Society* 24(5) (2010): 616–646. See also Shelley J. Correll, "Minimizing the Motherhood Penalty," Research Symposium, Gender and Work: Challenging Conventional Wisdom, Harvard Business School, 2013, accessed April 18, 2015, http://www.hbs.edu/faculty/conferences/2013-w50-research-symposium/Documents/correll.pdf.

29. Shelley J. Correll and Stephen Benard, "Getting a Job: Is There a Motherhood Penalty?" *American Journal of Sociology* 112(5) (2007): 1297–1339.

Chapter 2

1. Michael Inzlicht and Talia Ben-Zeev, "A Threatening Intellectual Environment: Why Females Are Susceptible to Experiencing Problem-Solving Deficits in the Presence of Males," *Psychological Science* 11(5) (2000): 365–371.

2. Toni Schmader and Alyssa Croft, "How Stereotypes Stifle Performance Potential," *Social and Personality Psychology Compass* 5(10) (2011): 792–806.

3. Schmader and Croft, "How Stereotypes Stifle Performance Potential."

4. Schmader and Croft, "How Stereotypes Stifle Performance Potential."

5. Michael Johns, Michael Inzlicht, and Toni Schmader, "Stereotype Threat and Executive Resource Depletion: Examining the Influence of Emotion Regulation," *Journal of Experimental Psychology: General* 137(4) (2008): 691–705.

6. Thomas E. Ford, Mark A. Ferguson, J. L. Brooks, K. M. Hagadone, "Coping Sense of Humor Reduces the Effect of Stereotype Threat on Women's Math Performance," *Personality and Social Psychology Bulletin* 30(5) (2004): 643–653.

7. Roxana Barbulescu and Matthew Bidwell, "Do Women Choose Different Jobs from Men? Mechanisms of Application Segregation in the Market for Managerial Workers," *Organization Science* 24(3) (2012): 737–756.

8. Barbulescu and Bidwell, "Do Women Choose Different Jobs from Men?"

9. Georges Desvaux, Sandrine Devillard-Hoellinger, and Mary C. Meaney, "A Business Case for Women," *McKinsey Quarterly*, September 2008, accessed June 24, 2015, http://www.talentnaardetop.nl/uploaded_files/document/2008_A _business_case_for_women.pdf.

10. Irene E. DePater, Annelies E. M. Van Vianen, Agneta H. Fischer, and Wendy P. Van Ginkel, "Challenging Experiences: Gender Differences in Task Choice," *Journal of Managerial Psychology* 24(1), 2009, 4–28.

11. Kathleen Connelly and Martin Heesacker, "Why Is Benevolent Sexism Appealing?: Associations with System Justification and Life Satisfaction," *Psychology of Women Quarterly* 36(4) (2012): 432–443.

12. Connelly and Heesacker, "Why Is Benevolent Sexism Appealing?: Associations With System Justification and Life Satisfaction."

13. Sarah Dinolfo, Christine Silva, and Nancy M. Carter, "High Potentials in the Pipeline: Leaders Pay It Forward," Catalyst, 2012, accessed August 12, 2015, http://www.catalyst.org/system/files/High_Potentials_In_the_Pipeline _Leaders_Pay_It_Forward.pdf.

14. 2014 WBI U.S. Workplace Bullying Survey, Workplace Bullying Institute. 2014, accessed August 12, 2015, http://workplacebullying.org/multi/pdf/2014-Survey-Flyer-B.pdf.

15. Hope Hodge Seck, "Controversy Surrounds Firing of Marines' Female Recruit Battalion CO," *Marine Times*, July 15, 2015, accessed September 20, 2015,

http://www.marinecorpstimes.com/story/military/2015/07/07/kate-germano
-fired-marine-corps-female-recruit-unit-commander/29763371/.

16. Leon Festinger, "A Theory of Social Comparison Processes," *Human Relations* 7(2) (1954): 117–140.

17. Faye Crosby, "The Denial of Personal Discrimination," *American Behavioral Scientist* 27(3) (1984): 371–386.

18. Mindi D. Foster and Micha Tsarfati, "The Effects of Meritocracy Beliefs on Women's Well-Being After First-Time Gender Discrimination," *Personality and Social Psychology Bulletin* 31(12) (2005): 1730–1738.

19. Christine Silva, Nancy M. Carter, Anna Beninger, "Good Intentions, Imperfect Execution? Women Get Fewer of the 'Hot Jobs' Needed to Advance," Catalyst, 2012, accessed June 24, 2015, http://www.catalyst.org/system/files/Good
_Intentions_Imperfect_Execution_Women_Get_Fewer_of_the_Hot_Jobs
_Needed_to_Advance.pdf.

Chapter 3

1. While we discuss a woman's ability to effectively manage the impressions she makes in terms of being able to use both communal and agentic behavior patterns, Professor Deborah Gruenfeld of Stanford Business School makes much the same point by talking about "playing low" and "playing high." While Gruenfeld is basically concerned with the projection of power by both women and men and does not concern herself explicitly with gender bias, she is very clear that when you want to exhibit power, you should "play high"—behave agenticly—and when you want to build personal connections, you should "play low"—behave communally. See Deborah Gruenfeld, "Playing High, Playing Low and Playing It Straight," YouTube, September 24, 2013, accessed September 28, 2015, https://www.youtube.com/watch?v=zbUX3BGXJlc&index=3&li
st=PL_I4p0xEPo8rXiClfU9vYlqwpAY0MYt3-.

2. Erving Goffman, *Presentation of Self in Everyday Life* (New York: Doubleday Anchor Books, 1959).

3. Val Singh, Savita Kumra, and Susan Vinnicombe, "Gender and Impression Management: Playing the Promotion Game," *Journal of Business Ethics* 37(1)(2002): 77–89. The researchers conducted two studies. In the first study they studied female U.K. business school graduates and their male peers to investigate the frequency with which they reported using impression management to advance their careers. In the second study, they conducted thirty-four in-depth interviews of consultants in a large international management consulting firm based in the U.K.

4. Olivia O'Neill and Charles O'Reilly III, "Reducing the Backlash Effect: Self-Monitoring and Women's Promotion," *Journal of Occupational and Organizational Psychology* 84(4) (2010): 825–832.

5. Sandy J. Wayne and Robert C. Liden, "Effects of Impression Management on Performance Ratings: A Longitudinal Study," *Academy of Management Journal* 38(1) (1995): 232–260. See also Singh, Kumra, and Vinnicombe, "Gender and Impression Management: Playing the Promotion Game," 78.

6. Francis J. Flynn and Daniel R. Ames, "What's Good for the Goose May Not Be As Good for the Gander: The Benefits of Self-Monitoring for Men and Women in Task Groups and Dyadic Conflicts," *Journal of Applied Psychology* 91(2) (2006): 272281. See also O'Neill and O'Reilly III, "Reducing the Backlash Effect: Self-Monitoring and Women's Promotion." 825-832.

7. Andrew J. Dubrin, *Impression Management in the Workplace: Research, Theory, and Practice* (Taylor & Francis, 2011).

8. Singh, Kumra, and Vinnicombe, "Gender and Impression Management: Playing the Promotion Game," 87.

9. Singh, Kumra, and Vinnicombe, "Gender and Impression Management: Playing the Promotion Game," 87.

10. Singh, Kumra, and Vinnicombe, "Gender and Impression Management: Playing the Promotion Game," 78.

11. Amy J. Cuddy, Matthew Kohut, and John Neffinger, "Connect, Then Lead," *Harvard Business Review* 91(78) (2013): 56.

Chapter 4

1. Malcolm Gladwell, *Outliers: The Story of Success* (New York: Little, Brown and Company, 2008).

2. J. K. Rowling, "The Fringe Benefits of Failure, and the Importance of Imagination," *Harvard Gazette,* accessed May 2, 2015, http://news.harvard.edu/gazette/story/2008/06/text-of-j-k-rowling-speech/.

3. Joshua Barajas, "Misty Copeland Makes History As American Ballet Theatre's First Black Principal Ballerina," *PBS NewsHour,* June 30, 2015, accessed September 28, 2015, http://www.pbs.org/newshour/rundown/misty-copeland-makes-history-first-female-african-american-principal-dancer/.

4. Lise Eliot, "Hardwired for Combat? First Female Army Ranger Graduates Prove Grit Beats Gender in Military Training," *Huffington Post,* August 31, 2015, accessed September 28, 2015, http://www.huffingtonpost.com/lise-eliot/hardwired-for-combat-first-female-army-ranger-graduates-prove-grit-beats-gender-in-military-training_b_8057094.html.

5. Milana Hogan, "Non-Cognitive Traits That Impact Female Success in Big Law," PhD diss., University of Pennsylvania, 2013.

6. Joanna Barsh and Lareina Yee, *Unlocking the Full Potential of Women at Work*, McKinsey & Company, accessed July 22, 2015, http://www.mckinsey.com/client_service/organization/latest_thinking/women_at_work.

7. "The Grit Project: True Grit and a Growth Mindset," American Bar Association, accessed May 2, 2015, http://www.americanbar.org/groups/women/initiatives _awards/grit.html.

8. Carol Dweck, *Mindset: The New Psychology of Success, How We Can Learn to Fulfill Our Potential* (New York: Ballantine Books, 2006).

9. Thomas E. Ford, Mark A. Ferguson, Jenna L. Brooks, and Kate M. Hagadone, "Coping Sense of Humor Reduces Effects of Stereotype Threat on Women's Math Performance," *Personality and Social Psychology Bulletin* 30(5) (2004): 643–653.

10. Nancy A. Yovetich, J. Alexander Dale, and Mary A. Hudak, "Benefits of Humor in Reduction of Threat-Induced Anxiety," *Psychological Reports* 66(1) (1990): 51–58.

11. Yovetich, Dale, and Hudak, "Benefits of Humor in Reduction of Threat-Induced Anxiety."

12. John A. Bargh, Mark Chen, and Laura Burrows, "Automaticity of Social Behavior: Direct Effects of Trait Construct and Stereotype Activation on Action," *Journal of Personality and Social Psychology* 71(2) (1996): 230–244; John A. Bargh, Annette Lee-Chai, Kimberly Barndollar, Peter M. Gollwitzer, and Roman Trötschel, "The Automated Will: Nonconscious Activation and Pursuit of Behavioral Goals," *Journal of Personality and Social Psychology* 81 (6) (2001): 1014–1017.

13. John R. Sparks, Charles S. Areni, and K. Chris Cox, "An Investigation of the Effects of Language Style and Communication Modality on Persuasion," *Communication Monographs* 65(2) (1998): 108–125.

14. Dana R. Carney, Judith A. Hall, and Lavonia Smith LeBeau, "Beliefs About the Nonverbal Expression of Social Power," *Journal of Nonverbal Behavior* 29(2) (2005): 105123; Judith A. Hall, Erik J. Coats, and Lavonia Smith LeBeau, "Nonverbal Behavior and the Vertical Dimension of Social Relations: A Meta-Analysis," *Psychological Bulletin* 131(6) (2005): 898924.

15. Nathanael J. Fast, Deborah H. Greenfield, Niro Sivanathan, and Adam D. Galinsky, "Illusory Control: A Generative Force Behind Power's Far-Reaching Effects," *Psychological Science* 20(4) (2009): 502–508; Cameron Anderson and Adam D. Galinsky, "Power, Optimism, and Risk-Taking," *European Journal of Social Psychology* 36 (2006): 511–536.

16. Joris Lammers, David Dubois, Derek D. Rucker, and Adam D. Galinsky, "Power Gets the Job: Priming Power Improves Interview Outcomes," *Journal of Experimental Social Psychology* 49(4) (2013): 776–779.

17. Adam D. Galinsky and Gavin J. Kilduff, "Be Seen As a Leader," *Harvard Business Review*, December 2013, accessed May 3, 2015, https://hbr.org/2013/12/ be-seen-as-a-leader.

18. Galinsky and Kilduff, "Be Seen As a Leader."

19. Amy Cuddy, "Your Body Language Shapes Who You Are," TED, accessed May 3, 2015, http://www.ted.com/talks/amy_cuddy_your_body_language_shapes _who_you_are.

20. Cuddy, "Your Body Language Shapes Who You Are."

21. Dana R. Carney, Amy J. C. Cuddy, and Andy J. Yap, "Power Posing: Brief Nonverbal Displays Affect Neuroendocrine Levels and Risk Tolerance," *Psychological Science* 21(10): 1363–1368; Julia Hanna, "Power Posing: Fake It Until You Make It," *Working Knowledge*, accessed May 3, 2015, http://hbswk.hbs.edu/ item/6461.html.

22. Carney, Cuddy, and Yap, "Power Posing."

Chapter 5

1. Linda L. Carli, Suzanne J. LeFleur, and Christopher C. Loeber, "Nonverbal Behavior, Gender, and Influence," *Journal of Personality and Social Psychology* 68(6) (1995): 1030–1041.

2. Carli, LeFleur, and Loeber, "Nonverbal Behavior, Gender, and Influence."

3. Alison R. Fragle, "The Power of Powerless Speech: The Effects of Speech Style and Task Interdependence on Status Conferral," *Organizational Behavior and Human Decision Processes* 101 (2006): 243–261.

4. Chris L. Kleinke, "Compliance to Requests Made by Gazing and Touching Experimenters in Field Settings," *Journal of Experimental Social Psychology* 13(3) (1977): 218–223.

5. April H. Crusco and Christopher G. Wetzel, "The Midas Touch: The Effects of Interpersonal Touch on Restaurant Tipping," *Personality and Social Psychology Bulletin* 10(4) (1984): 512–517; Amy S. Ebesu Hubbard, A. Allen Tsuji, Christine Williams, and Virgilio Seatriz Jr., "Effects of Touch on Gratuities Received in Same-Gender and Cross-Gender Dyads," *Journal of Applied Psychology* 33(11) (2003): 2427–2438.

6. Hajo Adam and Adam D. Galinsky, "Enclothed Cognition," *Journal of Experimental Social Psychology* 48(4) (2012): 918–925.

7. Adam and Galinsky, "Enclothed Cognition."

8. For a summary of the research on the relationships between a person's dress and how that affects the behavior of others toward that person, see Kim K. P. Johnson, Jeong-Ju Yoo, Minjeong Kim, Sharron J. Lennon, "Dress and Human Behavior: A Review and Critique," *Clothing & Textiles Research Journal* 26, no. 1 (2008): 3–22.

9. Take Ruth Bader Ginsburg, a justice on the U.S. Supreme Court, who is a force of nature. At five feet tall and maybe one hundred pounds, Ginsburg is a brave and principled woman who was turned down for a clerkship on the Supreme Court in 1960 because she was a woman. Ginsburg cofounded the first law journal that focused on women's rights, coauthored the first legal textbook on sex discrimination, and argued several landmark cases before the U.S. Supreme

Court, resulting in the end of legal gender discrimination in many areas of American law. *Forbes* recognized Ginsburg as one of the 100 Most Powerful Women (2009) and *Time* magazine named her one of the Time 100 icons (2015). Justice Ginsburg is brilliant and articulate. But watch her as she speaks; the woman is a forceful presence and always confident.

Chapter 6

1. David B. Duller, Beth A. LePoire, R. Kelly Aune, and Silvie V. Ely, "Social Perceptions As Mediators of the Effect of Speech Rate," *Human Communication Research* 19(2) (1992): 286311.

2. Angelina Jolie, "Angelina Jolie Speak[s] on World Refugee Day 2009," YouTube, June 20, 2009, accessed October 3, 2015, https://www.youtube.com/watch?v=qtt1Vs9Lcp0.

3. Douglas Quenqua, "They're Like, Way Ahead of the Linguistic Currrrve," *New York Times*, February 27, 2012, accessed June 8, 2015, http://www.nytimes.com/2012/02/28/science/young-women-often-trendsetters-in-vocal-patterns.html?_r=2&partner=rss&emc=rss&pagewanted=all.

4. Marc Lieberman, "Jill Abramson's Voice," *Language Log*, October 18, 2011, accessed June 8, 2015, http://languagelog.ldc.upenn.edu/nll/?p=3504.

5. Michael Saul, "Caroline Kennedy No Whiz with Words," *New York Daily News*, December 29, 2008, accessed May 20, 2015, http://www.nydailynews.com/news/politics/caroline-kennedy-no-whiz-words-article-1.355586.

6. Ellen Petry Leanse, "Google and Apple Alum Says Using This One Word Can Damage Your Credibility," *Business Insider*, June 25, 2015, accessed October 3, 2015, http://www.businessinsider.com/former-google-exec-says-this-word-can-damage-your-credibility-2015-6.

7. Rachel Simmons, *The Curse of the Good Girl: Raising Authentic Girls with Courage and Confidence* (New York: Penguin Books, 2009), 70. Simmons recognizes the excessive use of apologies among women as an attempt to appear communal, but warns that excessive apologies may cause women to adopt subordinate roles in their personal and professional lives.

8. "The Kardashians Talk Back to Tweets," YouTube, April 1, 2011, accessed October 3, 2015, https://www.youtube.com/watch?v=d8jL8qz7dwM.

9. Lindsey Stanberry, "Try This Experiment If You Say 'Sorry' Too Much," *Refinery 29*, August 3, 2015, accessed October 3, 2015, http://www.refinery29.com/saying-sorry-at-work#.ozt2o1:J1f7.

Chapter 7

1. Anthony Mulac, Karen T. Erlandson, W. Jeffrey Farrar, Jennifer S. Hallet, Jennifer L. Molloy, and Margaret Prescott, "Uh-huh. What's That All About?," *Communication Research* 25(6) (1998): 641–668.

2. Holly Weeks, "Taking the Stress out of Stressful Conversations," *Harvard Business Review*, July–August 2001, accessed June 24, 2015, https://hbr.org/2001/07/taking-the-stress-out-of-stressful-conversations.

3. Katharine Ridgway O'Brien, "Just Saying 'No': An Examination of Gender Differences in the Ability to Decline Requests in the Workplace," PhD diss., Rice University, 2014.

4. O'Brien, "Just Saying 'No': An Examination of Gender Differences in the Ability to Decline Requests in the Workplace."

5. Anne Kreamer, *It's Always Personal: Navigating Emotion in the New Workplace* (New York: Penguin, 2013).

6. Victoria L. Brescoll and Eric Luis Uhlmann, "Can an Angry Woman Get Ahead? Status Conferral, Gender, and Expression of Emotion in the Workplace," *Psychological Science* 19(3) (2008): 268–275.

7. Donald E. Gibson and Ronda Callister, "Anger in Organizations: Review and Future Directions" (paper presented at the 22nd Annual International Association of Conflict Management Conference, Kyoto, Japan, June 15–18, 2009).

8. Anne Karpf, *The Human Voice: How This Extraordinary Instrument Reveals Essential Clues About Who We Are* (New York: Bloomsbury USA, 2006), 55.

Chapter 8

1. Kathryn Heath, Jill Flynn, and Mary Davis Holt, "Women, Find Your Voice," *Harvard Business Review*, June 2014, accessed June 24, 2015, https://hbr.org/2014/06/women-find-your-voice.

2. Heath, Flynn, and Holt, "Women, Find Your Voice."

3. Adrienne B. Hancock and Benjamin A. Rubin, "Influence of Communication Partner's Gender on Language," *Journal of Language and Social Psychology* 34(1) (2015): 46–64.

4. Kristin J. Anderson and Campbell Leaper, "Meta-Analyses of Gender Effects on Conversational Interruption: Who, What, When, Where, and How," *Sex Roles* 39(3–4) (1998): 225–252.

5. Riana Duncan, "Excellent Suggestion, Miss Triggs," *Punch*, 1988.01.08.11.tif, available at http://punch.photoshelter.com/image/1000@HEXG1_wlmQ.

6. Leslie Perlow and Stephanie Williams, "Is Silence Killing Your Company?" *Engineering Management Review* 31(4) (2003): 18–23.

7. Christopher F. Karpowitz, Tali Mendelberg, and Lee Shaker, "Gender Inequality in Deliberative Participation," *American Political Science Review* 106(3) (2012): 533–547.

Chapter 9

1. Rachel Simmons, *The Curse of the Good Girl: Raising Authentic Girls with Courage and Confidence* (New York: Penguin, 2010).

2. Simmons, *The Curse of the Good Girl*, 102.

3. Joan C. Williams, "Hacking Tech's Diversity Problem," *Harvard Business Review*, October 2014, accessed September 13, 2015, https://hbr.org/2014/10/hacking-techs-diversity-problem.

4. Williams, "Hacking Tech's Diversity Problem."

5. Joyce F. Benenson, "The Development of Human Female Competition: Allies and Adversaries," *Philosophical Transactions of the Royal Society B: Biological Sciences* 368(1361) (2013): 1–11.

6. Benenson, "The Development of Human Female Competition."

7. Benenson, "The Development of Human Female Competition."

8. Julie E. Phelan, Corinne A. Moss-Racusin, and Laurie A. Rudman, "Competent Yet Out in the Cold: Shifting Criteria for Hiring Reflect Backlash Toward Agentic Women," *Psychology of Women Quarterly* 32 (4) (2008): 406–413.

9. Timothy A. Judge, Beth A. Livingston, and Charlice Hurst, "Do Nice Guys—and Gals—Really Finish Last? The Joint Effect of Sex and Agreeableness on Income," *Journal of Personality and Social Psychology* 102(2) (2012): 390–407; Madeline E. Heilman, "Gender Stereotypes and Workplace Bias," *Research in Organizational Behavior* 32 (2012): 113–135.

10. A recent study revealed that over half of working women believe they are overlooked for promotions because they are too modest, too reluctant to be clear and direct about their qualifications, too concerned about being seen as arrogant, big-headed, or pushy. See Laura Cummins, "Modesty Holding Women Back at Work," *Female First,* accessed September 13, 2015, http://www.femalefirst.co.uk/womens-issues/modesty-holding-women-back-at-work-543047.html.

11. Sarah J. Tracy and Kendra Dyanne Rivera, "Endorsing Equity and Applauding Stay at Home Moms: How Male Voices on Work–Life Reveal Aversive Sexism and Flickers of Transformation," *Management Communication Quarterly* 24(1) (2010): 3–43.

12. John Anderson, "The Film Fatales Collective Trains a Lens on Gender Inequality," *New York Times*, August 21, 2015, accessed September 13, 2015, http://www.nytimes.com/2015/08/23/movies/the-film-fatales-collective-trains-a-lens-on-gender-inequality.html?_r=0 (emphasis added).

13. Anderson, "The Film Fatales Collective Trains a Lens on Gender Inequality."

14. Olivia O'Neil and Charles O'Reilly III, "Reducing the Backlash Effect: Self-Monitoring and Women's Promotion," *Journal of Occupational and Organizational Psychology* 84(4) (2010): 825–832.

15. Shankar Vedantam, "Salary, Gender, and the Social Cost of Haggling," *Washington Post*, July 30, 2007, accessed September 13, 2015, http://www

.washingtonpost.com/wp-dyn/content/article/2007/07/29/AR200707
2900827.html.

16. Vedantam, "Salary, Gender, and the Social Cost of Haggling."

17. Juan M. Madera, Michelle R. Hebl, and Randi C. Martin, "Gender and Letters of Recommendation for Academia: Agentic and Communal Differences," *Journal of Applied Psychology*, 94(6): 1591–1599.

18. Madera, Hebl, and Martin, "Gender and Letters of Recommendation for Academia."

19. Madera, Hebl, and Martin, "Gender and Letters of Recommendation for Academia."

20. Laurie A. Rudman and Peter Glick, "Prescriptive Gender Stereotypes and Backlash Toward Agentic Women," *Journal of Social Issues* 57(4) (2001): 743–762.

21. Frances Trix and Carolyn Psenka, "Exploring the Color of Glass: Letters of Recommendation for Female and Male Medical Faculty," *Discourse & Society* 14(2) (2003): 191220.

Chapter 10

1. Sylvia Ann Hewlett, "Executive Women and the Myth of Having It All," *Harvard Business Review*, April 2002, accessed September 13, 2015, http://hbr.org/2002/04/executive-women-and-the-myth-of-having-it-all.

2. Anne Weisberg, "The Workplace Culture That Flying Nannies Won't Fix," *New York Times*, August 24, 2015, accessed September 13, 2015, http://www.nytimes.com/2015/08/24/opinion/the-workplace-culture-that-flying-nannies-wont-fix.html.

3. Hewlett, "Executive Women and the Myth of Having It All."

4. Rachel Thomas, "Corporate America Is Not on the Path to Gender Equality," Lean In, September 30, 2015, accessed October 4, 2015, http://leanin.org/news-inspiration/corporate-america-is-not-on-the-path-to-gender-equality/; McKinsey & Company, "Women in the Workplace," McKinsey & Company Insights & Publications, September 2015, accessed October 4, 2015, http://www.mckinsey.com/insights/organization/women_in_the_workplace.

5. Hannah Seligson, "Why the Sting of Layoffs Can Be Harder for Men," *New York Times*, January 31, 2009, accessed September 13, 2015, http://www.nytimes.com/2009/02/01/jobs/01layoff.html.

6. Jessica Grose, "It's Not Your Kids Holding Your Career Back. It's Your Husband," *Slate*, November 18, 2014, accessed September 13, 2015, http://www.slate.com/blogs/xx_factor/2014/11/18/harvard_business_school_study_it_s_not_kids_but_husbands_that_hold_women.html.

7. Claire Cain Miller, "Even Among Harvard Graduates, Women Fall Short of Their Work Expectations," *New York Times*, November 28, 2014, accessed September 13, 2015, http://www.nytimes.com/2014/11/30/upshot/even-among

-harvard-graduates-women-fall-short-of-their-work-expectations
.html.

8. Marianne Bertrand, Claudia Goldin, and Lawrence F. Katz, "Dynamics of the
   Gender Gap for Young Professionals in the Financial and Corporate Sectors,"
   American Economic Journal 2(3) (2010): 228–255.

9. Victoria Stilwell, "Fewer Millennial Moms Show U.S. Birth Rate Drop Lasting," *Bloomberg Business*, September 16, 2014, accessed September 13, 2015,
   http://www.bloomberg.com/news/articles/2014-09-16/fewer-millennial-moms
   -show-u-s-birth-rate-drop-lasting.

10. Claire Cain Miller, "The Motherhood Penalty vs. the Fatherhood Bonus: A
    Child Helps Your Career, If You're a Man," *New York Times*, September 6, 2014,
    accessed September 13, 2015, http://www.nytimes.com/2014/09/07/upshot/
    a-child-helps-your-career-if-youre-a-man.html; Shelley J. Correll and Stephen
    Benard, "Getting a Job: Is There a Motherhood Penalty?" *American Journal of
    Sociology* 112(5) (2007): 1297–1339.

11. Miller, "The Motherhood Penalty vs. the Fatherhood Bonus."

12. Miller, "Even Among Harvard Graduates, Women Fall Short of Their
    Work Expectations."

13. Katharine Zaleski, "Female Company President: 'I'm Sorry to All the Mothers
    I Worked With,'" *Fortune*, March 3, 2015, accessed September 13, 2015,
    http://fortune.com/2015/03/03/female-company-president-im-sorry-to-all-the
    -mothers-i-used-to-work-with/.

14. Kim Parker and Wendy Wang, "Modern Parenthood: Roles of Moms
    and Dads Converge As They Balance Work and Family," Pew Research
    Center, March 14, 2013, accessed September 13, 2015, http://www
    .pewsocialtrends.org/2013/03/14/modern-parenthood-roles-of-moms-and
    -dads-converge-as-they-balance-work-and-family/.

15. George Gao and Gretchen Livingston, "Working While Pregnant Is Much
    More Common Than It Used to Be," Pew Research Center, March 31, 2015,
    accessed September 13, 2015, http://www.pewresearch.org/fact-tank/2015/
    03/31/working-while-pregnant-is-much-more-common-than-it-used-to-be/.

16. Gao and Livingston, "Working While Pregnant Is Much More Common Than
    It Used to Be"; Bourree Lam, "Yes, There Really Are More Pregnant Women
    in the Office," *Atlantic*, April 8, 2015, accessed September 13, 2015, http://
    www.theatlantic.com/business/archive/2015/04/yes-there-really-are-more
    -pregnant-women-at-the-office/389763/.

17. Melissa A. Milkie, Kei A. Nomaguchi, and Kathleen E. Denny, "Does the
    Amount of Time Mothers Spend with Children or Adolescents Matter?" *Journal
    of Marriage and Family* 77(2) (2015): 355–372.

18. Milkie, Nomaguchi, and Denny, "Does the Amount of Time Mothers Spend
    with Children or Adolescents Matter?"

19. Terri LeMoyne and Tom Buchanan, "Does 'Hovering' Matter? Helicopter Parenting and Its Effect on Well-Being," *Sociological Spectrum* 31(4) (2011): 399–418; Chris Segrin, Alesia Woszidlo, Michelle Givertz, and Neil Montgomery, "Parent and Child Traits Associated with Overparenting," *Journal of Social and Clinical Psychology* 32(6): 569–595; Holly H. Schifferin, Miriam Liss, Haley Miles McLean et al., "Helping or Hovering? The Effects of Helicopter Parenting on College Students' Well-Being," *Journal of Child and Family Studies* 23(3) (2014): 548–557.

20. Julie Lythcott-Haims, *How to Raise an Adult: Break Free of the Overparenting Trap and Prepare Your Kid for Success* (New York: Henry Holt and Company, 2015).

21. Julie Lythcott-Haims, "Kids of Helicopter Parents Are Sputtering Out," *Slate*, July 5, 2015, accessed September 13, 2015, http://www.slate.com/articles/double_x/doublex/2015/07/helicopter_parenting_is_increasingly_correlated_with_college_age_depression.html.

22. Carmen Nobel, "Kids Benefit from Having a Working Mom," *HBS Working Knowledge*, May 15, 2015, accessed September 13, 2015, http://hbswk.hbs.edu/item/7791.html.

23. Nobel, "Kids Benefit from Having a Working Mom."

24. Mauro Whiteman, "PepsiCo CEO Indra Nooyi: 'I Don't Think Women Can Have It All Either,'" *Aspen Idea Blog,* July 1, 2014, accessed September 13, 2015, http://www.aspeninstitute.org/about/blog/pepsico-ceo-indra-nooyi-i-don-t-think-women-can-have-it-all-either.

25. Matthew Sparkes, "Christine Lagarde: 'Women Can't Have It All,'" *Business Insider*, September 26, 2012, accessed September 13, 2015, http://www.businessinsider.com/christine-lagarde-women-cant-have-it-all-2012-9.

26. Taffy Brodesser-Akner, "Drew Barrymore: The Unexpected Supermogul," *More*, accessed September 13, 2015, http://www.more.com/entertainment/celebrities-movies-tv-music/drew-barrymore-unexpected-supermogul-more-magazine-february-2015-cover.

27. Anne-Marie Slaughter, "Why Women Still Can't Have It All," *Atlantic*, July/August 2012, accessed September 13, 2015, http://www.theatlantic.com/magazine/archive/2012/07/why-women-still-cant-have-it-all/309020/.

28. Slaughter, "Why Women Still Can't Have It All."

REFERENCES

Adam, Hajo, and Adam D. Galinsky. "Enclothed Cognition." *Journal of Experimental Social Psychology* 48(4) (2012): 918–925.

Agars, Mark D. "Reconsidering the Impact of Gender Stereotypes on the Advancement of Women in Organizations." *Psychology of Women Quarterly* 28(2) (2004): 103–111.

Anderson, Cameron, and Adam D. Galinsky. "Power, Optimism, and Risk-Taking." *European Journal of Social Psychology* 36(4) (2006): 511–536.

Anderson, John. "The Film Fatales Collective Trains a Lens on Gender Inequality." *New York Times*, August 21, 2015. Accessed September 13, 2015. http://www.nytimes.com/2015/08/23/movies/the-film-fatales-collective-trains-a-lens-on-gender-inequality.html?_r=0.

Anderson, Kristin J., and Campbell Leaper. "Meta-Analyses of Gender Effects on Conversational Interruption: Who, What, When, Where, and How." *Sex Roles* 39(3–4) (1998): 225–252.

"As Academic Gender Gap Declines, There Is Still Work to be Done." *Harbus*, April 25, 2011. Accessed June 7, 2015. http://www.harbus.org/2011/gender-gap/.

Babcock, Linda, and Sara Laschever. *Women Don't Ask: Negotiation and the Gender Divide*. Princeton: Princeton University Press, 2003.

Banaji, Mahzarin, and Anthony Greenwald. *Blindspot: Hidden Biases of Good People*. New York: Delacorte Press, 2013.

Barajas, Joshua. "Misty Copeland Makes History As American Ballet Theatre's First Black Principal Ballerina." *PBS NewsHour,* June 30, 2015. Accessed September 28, 2015. http://www.pbs.org/newshour/rundown/misty-copeland-makes-history-first-female-african-american-principal-dancer/.

Barbulescu, Roxana, and Matthew Bidwell. "Do Women Choose Different Jobs from Men? Mechanisms of Application Segregation in the Market for Managerial Workers." *Organization Science* 24(3) (2012): 737–756.

Bargh, John A., Annette Lee-Chai, Kimberly Barndollar, Peter M. Gollwitzer, and Roman Trötschel. "The Automated Will: Nonconscious Activation and Pursuit of Behavioral Goals." *Journal of Personality and Social Psychology* 81(6) (2001): 1014–1027.

Bargh, John A., Mark Chen, and Lara Burrows. "Automaticity of Social Behavior: Direct Effects of Trait Construct and Stereotype Activation on Action." *Journal of Personality and Social Psychology* 71(2) (1996): 230–244.

Barsh, Joanna, and Lareina Yee. *Unlocking the Full Potential of Women at Work.* McKinsey & Company. Accessed July 22, 2015. http://www.mckinsey.com/client_service/organization/latest_thinking/women_at_work.

Baxter, Judith. "Women of the Corporation: A Sociological Perspective of Senior Women's Leadership Language in the U.K." *Journal of Sociolinguistics* 16(1) (2012): 81–107.

Bem, Sandra L. "The Measurement of Psychological Androgyny." *Journal of Consulting and Clinical Psychology* 42 (1981): 155–162.

Benenson, Joyce F. "The Development of Human Female Competition: Allies and Adversaries." *Philosophical Transactions of the Royal Society of Biological Sciences* 368(1361) (2013): 1–11.

Benard, Stephen, and Shelley J. Correll. "Normative Discrimination and the Motherhood Penalty." *Gender and Society* 24(5) (2010): 616–646.

Bertrand, Marianne, Claudia Goldin, and Lawrence F. Katz. "Dynamics of the Gender Gap for Young Professionals in the Financial and Corporate Sectors." *American Economic Journal* 2(3) (2010): 228–255.

Biernat, Monica, M. J. Tocci, and Joan C. Williams. "The Language of Performance Evaluations: Gender-Based Shifts in Content and Consistency of Judgment." *Social Psychology and Personality Science* 3(2) (2012): 186–192.

Brescoll, Victoria L., and Eric Luis Uhlmann. "Can an Angry Woman Get Ahead? Status Conferral, Gender, and Expression of Emotion in the Workplace." *Psychological Science* 19(3) (2008): 268–275.

Brinol, Pablo, Richard E. Petty, and Benjamin Wagner. "Body Posture Effects on Self-Evaluation: A Self-Validation Approach." *European Journal of Social Psychology* 39 (2009): 1053–1064.

Brodesser-Akner, Taffy. "Drew Barrymore: The Unexpected Supermogul." *MORE.* Accessed September 13, 2015. http://www.more.com/entertainment/celebrities-movies-tv-music/drew-barrymore-unexpected-supermogul-more-magazine-february-2015-cover.

Caraher, Lee. *Millennials & Management: The Essential Guide to Making It Work at Work.* Brookline, MA: Bibliomotion, Inc., 2015.

Carli, Linda L., Suzanne J. LaFleur, and Christopher C. Loeber. "Nonverbal Behavior, Gender, and Influence." *Journal of Personality and Social Psychology* 68(6) (1995): 1030–1041.

Carney, Dana R., Amy J. C. Cuddy, and Andy J. Yap. "Power Posing: Brief Nonverbal Displays Affect Neuroendocrine Levels and Risk Tolerance." *Psychological Science* 21(10) (2010): 1363–1368.

Carney, Dana R., Judith A. Hall, and Lavonia S. LeBeau. "Beliefs About the Nonverbal Expression of Social Power." *Journal of Nonverbal Behavior* 29(2) (2005): 105–123.

Carter, Nancy M., and Christine Silva. "Mentoring: Necessary but Insufficient for Advancement." Catalyst (2010). Accessed August 8, 2015. http://www.catalyst .org/system/files/Mentoring_Necessary_But_Insufficient_for_Advancement _Final_120610.pdf

Connelly, Kathleen, and Martin Heesacker. "Why Is Benevolent Sexism Appealing?: Associations with System Justification and Life Satisfaction." *Psychology of Women Quarterly* 36(4) (2012): 432–443.

Correll, Shelley J. "Minimizing the Motherhood Penalty." Research Symposium, Gender and Work: Challenging Conventional Wisdom, Harvard Business School, 2013. Accessed June 7, 2015. http://www.hbs.edu/faculty/conferences/ 2013-w50-research-symposium/Documents/correll.pdf.

Correll, Shelley J., and Stephen Benard. "Getting a Job: Is There a Motherhood Penalty?" *American Journal of Sociology* 112(5) (2007): 1297–1339.

Costa, Marco, Marzia Menzani, and Pio Eprico Ricci Bitti. "Head Canting in Paintings: An Historical Study." *Journal of Nonverbal Behavior* 25(1) (2001): 63–73.

Crosby, Faye. "The Denial of Personal Discrimination." *American Behavioral Scientist* 27(3) (1984): 371–386.

Crusco, April H., and Christopher G. Wetzel. "The Midas Touch: The Effects of Interpersonal Touch on Restaurant Tipping." *Personality and Social Psychology Bulletin* 10(4) (1984): 512–517.

Cuddy, Amy. "Your Body Language Shapes Who You Are." TED Global 2012, June 2012. Accessed June 7, 2015. http://www.ted.com/talks/amy_cuddy_your_body _language_shapes_who_you_are.

Cuddy, Amy J. C., Matthew Kohut, and John Neffinger. "Connect, Then Lead." *Harvard Business Review* 9, no. 17–8 (2013): 54–61.

Cummins, Laura. "Modesty Holding Women Back at Work," Female First. Accessed September 13, 2015. http://www.femalefirst.co.uk/womens-issues/modesty -holding-women-back-at-work-543047.html.

Dardenne, Benoit, Muriel Dumont, and Thierry Bonier. "Insidious Dangers of Benevolent Sexism: Consequences for Women's Performance." *Journal of Personality and Social Psychology* 93(5) (2007): 764–779.

De Pater, Irene E., Annelies E. M. Van Vianen, Agneta H. Fischer, and Wendy P. Van Ginkel. "Challenging Experiences: Gender Differences in Task Choice." *Journal of Managerial Psychology* 24(1) (2009): 4–28.

Desai, Sreedhari D., Dolly Chugh, and Arthur P. Brief. "The Organizational Implications of a Traditional Marriage: Can a Domestic Traditionalist by Night Be an Organizational Egalitarian by Day?" UNC Kenan-Flagler Research Paper No. 2013-19, March 12, 2012. Accessed June 6, 2015. http://papers.ssrn.com/sol3/ papers.cfm?abstract_id=2018259##.

Desvaux, Georges, Sandrine Devillard-Hoellinger, and Mary C. Meaney. "A Business Case for Women." *McKinsey Quarterly* (September 2008). Accessed June 24, 2015. http://www.talentnaardetop.nl/uploaded_files/document/2008_A _business_case_for_women.pdf.

Dinolfo, Sarah, Christine Silva, and Nancy M. Carter. "High Potentials in the Pipeline: Leaders Pay It Forward." Catalyst (2012). Accessed August 8, 2015. http:// www.catalyst.org/system/files/High_Potentials_In_the_Pipeline_Leaders _Pay_It_Forward.pdf.

"Dove Campaign for Real Beauty." Accessed June 7, 2015. http://www.dove.us/ Social-Mission/campaign-for-real-beauty.aspx.

Dubrin, Andrew J. *Impression Management in the Workplace: Research, Theory and Practice.* New York: Taylor & Francis, 2010.

Duller, David B., Beth A. LePoire, R. Kelly Aune, and Silvie V. Eloy. "Social Perceptions As Mediators of the Effect of Speech Rate." *Human Communication Research* 19(2) (1992): 286–311.

Dweck, Carol S. *Mindset: The New Psychology of Success.* New York: Ballantine Books, 2006.

Eliot, Lise. "Hardwired for Combat? First Female Army Ranger Graduates Prove Grit Beats Gender in Military Training." *Huffington Post,* August 31, 2015. Accessed September 28, 2015. http://www.huffingtonpost.com/lise-eliot/hardwired-for -combat-first-female-army-ranger-graduates-prove-grit-beats-gender-in-military -training_b_8057094.html.

Fast, Nathanael J., Deborah H. Gruenfeld, Niro Sivanathan, and Adam D. Galinsky. "Illusory Control: A Generative Force Behind Power's Far-Reaching Effects." *Psychological Science* 20(4) (2009): 502–508.

Festinger, Leon. "A Theory of Social Comparison Processes." *Human Relations* 7(2) (1954): 117–140.

Ford, Cecilia E. *Women Speaking Up: Getting and Using Turns in Workplace Meetings.* London: Palgrave Macmillan, 2008.

Ford, Thomas E., Mark A. Ferguson, Jenna L. Brooks, and Kate M. Hagadone. "Coping Sense of Humor Reduces Effects of Stereotype Threat on Women's Math Performance." *Personality and Social Psychology Bulletin* 30(5) (2004): 643–653.

Foster, Mindi D., and Micha Tsarfati. "The Effects of Meritocracy Beliefs on Women's Well-Being After First-Time Gender Discrimination." *Personality and Social Psychology Bulletin* 31(12) (2005): 1730–1738.

Flynn, Francis J., and Daniel R. Ames. "What's Good for the Goose May Not Be As Good for the Gander: The Benefits of Self-Monitoring for Men and Women in Task Groups and Dyadic Conflicts." *Journal of Applied Psychology* 91(2) (2006): 272–281.

Friedman, Ann. "Martha Stewart's Best Lesson: Don't Give a Damn." *New York Magazine,* March 14, 2013. Accessed June 7, 2015. http://nymag.com/ thecut/2013/03/martha-stewarts-best-lesson-dont-give-a-damn.html.

Galinsky, Adam D., and Gavin J. Kilduff. "Be Seen As a Leader." *Harvard Business Review*, December 1, 2013. Accessed June 7, 2015. https://hbr.org/2013/12/be-seen-as-a-leader.

Gangestad, Steven W., and Mark Snyder. "Self-Monitoring: Appraisal and Reappraisal." *Psychological Bulletin* 126(4) (2000): 530–555.

Gao, George, and Gretchen Livingston. "Working While Pregnant Is Much More Common Than It Used to Be." Pew Research Center, March 31, 2015. Accessed September 13, 2015. http://www.pewresearch.org/fact-tank/2015/03/31/working-while-pregnant-is-much-more-common-than-it-used-to-be/.

Gawande, Atul. "Personal Best." *New Yorker*, October 3, 2011. Accessed June 7, 2015. http://www.newyorker.com/magazine/2011/10/03/personal-best.

Gibson, Donald E., and Ronda Callister. "Anger in Organizations: Review and Future Directions." Paper presented at the 22nd Annual International Association of Conflict Management Conference, Kyoto, Japan, June 15–18, 2009.

Gladwell, Malcolm. *Outliers: The Story of Success*. New York: Little, Brown and Company, 2008.

Gladwell, Malcolm. "Teens' Language Is, Like, Sooo Influential." *The Milwaukee Sentinel*, June 6, 1992.

Glick, Peter, and Susan T. Fiske. "The Ambivalent Sexism Inventory: Differentiating Hostile and Benevolent Sexism." *Journal of Personality and Social Psychology* 70(3) (1996): 491–512.

Goffman, Erving. *The Presentation of Self in Everyday Life*. New York: Doubleday Anchor Books, 1959.

Grose, Jessica. "It's Not Your Kids Holding Your Career Back. It's Your Husband." *Slate*, November 18, 2014. Accessed September 13, 2015. http://www.slate.com/blogs/xx_factor/2014/11/18/harvard_business_school_study_it_s_not_kids_but_husbands_that_hold_women.html.

Gruenfeld, Deborah. "Playing High, Playing Low and Playing It Straight." YouTube, September 24, 2013. Accessed September 28, 2015. https://www.youtube.com/watch?v=zbUX3BGXJlc&index=3&list=PL_I4p0xEPo8rXiClfU9vYlqwpAY0MYt3-.

Hall, Judith A., Erik J. Coats, and Lavonia S. LeBeau. "Nonverbal Behavior and the Vertical Dimension of Social Relations: A Meta-Analysis." *Psychological Bulletin* 131(6) (2005): 898–924.

Hammill, Greg. "Mixing and Managing Four Generations of Employees." *FDU Magazine Online*, 2005. Accessed June 7, 2015. http://www.fdu.edu/newspubs/magazine/05ws/generations.htm.

Hancock, Adrienne B., and Benjamin A. Rubin. "Influence of Communication Partner's Gender on Language." *Journal of Language and Social Psychology* 34(1) (2015): 46–64.

Handbook of Career Theory, edited by Michael B. Arthur, Douglas T. Hall, and Barbara Lawrence. Cambridge: University Press, 1989.

Hanna, Julia. "Power Posing: Fake It Until You Make It." *Working Knowledge*, September 20, 2010. Accessed June 7, 2015. http://hbswk.hbs.edu/item/6461.html.

Harris, Russ. *The Confidence Gap: A Guide to Overcoming Fear and Self-Doubt.* Boston: Trumpeter Books, 2011.

Heath, Kathryn, Jill Flynn, and Mary Davis Holt. "Women, Find Your Voice." *Harvard Business Review*, June 2014. Accessed June 24, 2015. https://hbr.org/2014/06/women-find-your-voice.

Heilman, Madeline E. "Gender Stereotypes and Workplace Bias." *Research in Organizational Behavior* 32 (2012): 113–135.

Hewlett, Sylvia Ann. "Executive Women and the Myth of Having It All." *Harvard Business Review*, April 2002. Accessed September 13, 2015. http://hbr.org/2002/04/executive-women-and-the-myth-of-having-it-all.

Hogan, Milana L. "Non-Cognitive Traits That Impact Female Success in Big Law." PhD diss., University of Pennsylvania, 2013.

Hubbard, Amy S., A. Allen Tsuji, Christine Williams, and Virgilio Seatriz Jr., "Effects of Touch on Gratuities Received in Same-Gender and Cross-Gender Dyads," *Journal of Applied Psychology* 33(11) (2003): 2427–2438.

Hume, David. "Of the Standard of Taste." In *The Philosophical Works of David Hume: Including All the Essays and Exhibiting the More Important Alterations and Corrections in the Successive Editions Published By the Author.* Vol. 3. Boston: Little, Brown and Company, 1914.

"In the Archives: Abraham Lincoln and the Emancipation Diversion (1862)." Humor in America, February 21, 2013. Accessed June 7, 2015. https://humorinamerica.wordpress.com/2013/02/21/in-the-archives-lincoln-diversion-1862/.

Inzlicht, Michael, and Talia Ben-Zeev. "A Threatening Intellectual Environment: Why Females Are Susceptible to Experiencing Problem-Solving Deficits in the Presence of Males." *Psychological Science* 11(5) (2000): 365–371.

Jolie, Angelina. "Angelina Jolie Speak[s] on World Refugee Day 2009." United Nations High Commissioner for Refugees, June 20, 2009. Accessed October 3, 2015. https://www.youtube.com/watch?v=qtt1Vs9Lcp0.

Johns, Michael, Michael Inzlicht, and Toni Schmader. "Stereotype Threat and Executive Resource Depletion: Examining the Influence of Emotion Regulation." *Journal of Experimental Psychology: General* 137(4) (2008): 691–705.

Johnson, Kim. K. P., Jeong-Ju Yoo, Minjeong Kim, and Sharron J. Lennon. "Dress and Human Behavior: A Review and Critique." *Clothing & Textiles Research Journal* 26(1) (2008): 3–22.

Judge, Timothy A., Beth A. Livingston, and Charlice Hurst. "Do Nice Guys—and Gals—Really Finish Last? The Joint Effect of Sex and Agreeableness on Income." *Journal of Personality and Social Psychology* 102(2) (2012): 390–407.

Kantor, Jodi. "Harvard Business School Case Study: Gender Equity." *New York Times*, September 7, 2013. Accessed June 6, 2015. http://www.nytimes.com /2013/09/08/education/harvard-case-study-gender-equity.html?pagewanted =all&_r=0.

Karpf, Anne. *The Human Voice: How This Extraordinary Instrument Reveals Essential Clues About Who We Are.* New York: Bloomsbury USA, 2006.

Karpowitz, Christopher, F. Tali Mendelberg, and Lee Shaker. "Gender Inequality in Deliberative Participation." *American Political Science Review* 106(3) (2012): 533–547.

Kilduff, Martin, and David V. Day. "Do Chameleons Get Ahead? The Effects of Self-Monitoring on Managerial Careers." *Academy of Management Journal* 37(4) (1994): 1047–1060.

King, Eden B., Whitney Botsford, Michelle R. Hebl, Stephanie Kazama, Jeremy F. Dawson, and Andrew Perkins. "Benevolent Sexism at Work: General Differences in the Distribution of Challenging Developmental Experiences." *Journal of Management* 38(6) (2012): 1835–1866.

Kleinke, Chris L. "Compliance to Requests Made by Gazing and Touching Experimenters in Field Settings." *Journal of Experimental Social Psychology* 13(3) (1977): 218–223.

Kolb, Deborah M., Judith Williams, and Carol Frohlinger. *Her Place at the Table: A Woman's Guide to Negotiating Five Key Challenges to Leadership Success.* San Francisco: Jossey-Bass, 2010.

Kramer, Andrea S. "Additional Things Women Can Do For Themselves." *Women's Bar Association of Illinois Newsletter* (2011).

Kramer, Andrea S. "Bragging Rights: Self-Evaluation Dos and Don'ts." *Women Lawyers Journal* (2007).

Kramer, Andrea S. "Professional Advancement and Gender Stereotypes: The 'Rules' for Better Gender Communications." *Women's Bar Association of Illinois Newsletter* (2011).

Kramer, Andrea S. "Self-Evaluations: Dos and Don'ts." *Women's Bar Association of Illinois Newsletter* (2011).

Kramer, Andrea S. "What Professional Organizations Should Do To Advance Their Women Leaders." *Women's Bar Association of Illinois Newsletter* (2011).

Kramer, Andrea S., and Alton B. Harris. "Taking Control: Women, Gender Stereotypes and Impression Management." *Women's Bar Association of Illinois Newsletter* (2014).

Kramer, Andrea S., Carol Frohlinger, and Jane DiRenzo Pigott. *What You Need to Know About Negotiating Compensation.* American Bar Association, June 18, 2013. Accessed June 6, 2015. http://www.americanbar.org/content/ dam/aba/administrative/women/negotiations_guide_task_force.authcheck dam.pdf.

Kramer, Andrea S., Lisa B. Horowitz, Sharon Meit Abrahams, and Susan Smith Ross. "The Design, Development and Implementation of a Women's Initiative." *Managing Partner Magazine*, 2007.

Kreamer, Anne. *It's Always Personal: Navigating Emotion in the New Workplace*. New York: Penguin, 2013.

Kulik, Carol T., and Mana Olekalns. "Negotiating the Gender Divide: Lessons from the Negotiation and Organizational Behavior Literatures." *Journal of Management* 38(4) (2012): 1387–1415.

LaFrance, Marianne, Marvin A. Hecht, and Elizabeth Levy Paluck. "The Contingent Smile: A Meta-Analysis of Sex Differences in Smiling." *Psychological Bulletin* 129(2) (2003): 305–334.

Lakoff, Robin T. *Language and Woman's Place*. Cambridge: Cambridge University Press, 1975.

Lam, Bourree. "Yes, There Really Are More Pregnant Women in the Office." *Atlantic*, April 8, 2015. Accessed September 13, 2015. http://www.theatlantic.com/business/archive/2015/04/yes-there-really-are-more-pregnant-women-at-the-office/389763/.

Lammers, Joris, David Dubois, Derek D. Rucker, and Adam D. Galinsky. "Power Gets the Job: Priming Power Improves Interview Outcomes." *Journal of Experimental Social Psychology* 49(4) (2013): 776–779.

Leanse, Ellen Petry. "Google and Apple Alum Says Using This One Word Can Damage Your Credibility." *Business Insider,* June 25, 2015. Accessed October 3, 2015. http://www.businessinsider.com/former-google-exec-says-this-word-can-damage-your-credibility-2015-6.

Lieberman, Marc. "Jill Abramson's Voice." *Language Log,* October 18, 2011. Accessed June 8, 2015. http://languagelog.ldc.upenn.edu/nll/?p=3504.

LeMoyne, Terri and Tom Buchanan. "Does 'Hovering' Matter? Helicopter Parenting and Its Effect on Well-Being." *Sociological Spectrum* 31(4) (2011): 399–418.

Lythcott-Haims, Julie. *How to Raise an Adult: Break Free of the Overparenting Trap and Prepare Your Kid for Success*. New York: Henry Holt and Company, 2015.

Lythcott-Haims, Julie. "Kids of Helicopter Parents Are Sputtering Out." *Slate*, July 5, 2015. Accessed September 13, 2015. http://www.slate.com/articles/double_x/doublex/2015/07/helicopter_parenting_is_increasingly_correlated_with_college_age_depression.html.

Madera, Juan M., Michelle R. Hebl, and Randi C. Martin. "Gender and Letters of Recommendation for Academia: Agentic and Communal Differences." *Journal of Applied Psychology* 94(6): 1591–1599.

McKinsey & Company. "Women in the Workplace." McKinsey & Company Insights & Publications, September 2015. Accessed October 4, 2015. http://www.mckinsey.com/insights/organization/women_in_the_workplace.

Milkie, Melissa A., Kei A. Nomaguchi, and Kathleen E. Denny. "Does the Amount of Time Mothers Spend with Children or Adolescents Matter?" *Journal of Marriage and Family* 77(2) (2015): 355–372.

Miller, Claire Cain. "Even Among Harvard Graduates, Women Fall Short of Their Work Expectations." *New York Times*, November 28, 2014. Accessed September 13, 2015. http://www.nytimes.com/2014/11/30/upshot/even-among-harvard-graduates-women-fall-short-of-their-work-expectations.html.

Miller, Claire Cain. "The Motherhood Penalty vs. the Fatherhood Bonus: A Child Helps Your Career, If You're a Man." *New York Times*, September 6, 2014. Accessed September 13, 2015. http://www.nytimes.com/2014/09/07/upshot/a-child-helps-your-career-if-youre-a-man.html.

Minsberg, Talya. "Women Describe Their Struggles with Gender Roles in Military." *New York Times,* May 24, 2015. Accessed June 24, 2015. http://www.nytimes.com/2015/05/25/health/women-describe-their-struggles-with-gender-roles-in-military.html.

Moss-Racusin, Corinne A., John F. Dovidio, Victoria L. Brescoll, Mark J. Graham, and Jo Handelsman. "Science Faculty's Subtle Gender Biases Favor Male Students." *PNAS* 109(41) (2012): 16474–16479.

Mulac, Anthony, Karen T. Erlandson, W. Jeffrey Farrar, Jennifer S. Hallet, Jennifer L. Molloy, and Margaret Prescott. "Uh-huh. What's That All About?" *Communication Research* 25(6) (1998): 641–668.

Nobel, Carmen. "Kids Benefit from Having a Working Mom." *HBS Working Knowledge,* May 15, 2015. Accessed September 13, 2015. http://hbswk.hbs.edu/item/7791.html.

O'Brien, Katharine Ridgway. "Just Saying 'No': An Examination of Gender Differences in the Ability to Decline Requests in the Workplace." PhD. diss., Rice University, 2014.

O'Grady, Kim. "How I Discovered Gender Discrimination." *What Would King Leonidas Do?,* July 9, 2013. Accessed June 6, 2015. http://whatwouldkingleonidasdo.tumblr.com/post/54989171152/how-i-discovered-gender-discrimination.

O'Neill, Olivia, and Charles O'Reilly III. "Reducing the Backlash Effect: Self-Monitoring and Women's Promotion." *Journal of Occupational and Organizational Psychology* 84(4) (2011): 825–832.

Palomares, Nicholas A. "Women Are Sort of More Tentative Than Men, Aren't They?: How Men and Women Use Tentative Language Differently, Similarly, and Counterstereotypically As a Function of Gender Salience." *Communication Research* 36(4) (2009): 538–560.

Park, Ryan. "What Ruth Bader Ginsburg Taught Me About Being a Stay-at-Home Dad." *Atlantic,* January 8, 2015. Accessed June 6, 2015. http://www.theatlantic.com/business/archive/2015/01/what-ruth-bader-ginsburg-taught-me-about-being-a-stay-at-home-dad/384289/.

Parker, Kim, and Wendy Wang. "Modern Parenthood: Roles of Moms and Dads Converge As They Balance Work and Family." Pew Research Center, March 14, 2013. Accessed September 13, 2015. http://www.pewsocialtrends.org/2013/03/14/ modern-parenthood-roles-of-moms-and-dads-converge-as-they-balance-work -and-family/.

Pershing LLC. "Americans Crave a New Kind of Leader—and Women Are Ready to Deliver." February 25, 2014. Accessed June 6, 2015. https://www.pershing. com/our-thinking/thought-leadership/americans-crave-a-new-kind-of-leader -and-women-are-ready-to-deliver.

Phelan, Julie E., Corinne A. Moss-Racusin, and Laurie A. Rudman. "Competent Yet Out in the Cold: Shifting Criteria for Hiring Reflect Backlash Toward Agentic Women." *Psychology of Women Quarterly* 32 (4) (2008): 406–413.

Prentice, Deborah A., and Erica Carranza. "What Women and Men Should Be, Shouldn't Be, Are Allowed to Be, and Don't Have to Be: The Contents of Prescriptive Gender Stereotypes." *Psychology of Women Quarterly* 26(4) (2002): 279–280.

Prime, Jeanine, and Corinne A. Moss-Rasusin. "Engaging Men in Gender Initiatives: What Change Agents Need to Know." Catalyst, May 4, 2009. Accessed September 19, 2015. http://www.catalyst.org/knowledge/engaging -men-gender-initiatives-what-change-agents-need-know.

Rhode, Deborah. *What Women Want: An Agenda for the Women's Movement.* Oxford: Oxford University Press, 2014.

Ridgeway, Cecilia L. *Framed by Gender: How Gender Inequality Persists in the Modern World.* New York: Oxford University Press, 2011.

Rigoglioso, Marguerite. "Researchers: How Women Can Succeed in the Workplace." *Insights by Stanford Business,* March 1, 2011. Accessed June 7, 2015. http://www .gsb.stanford.edu/insights/researchers-how-women-can-succeed-workplace.

Rowling, J. K. "The Fringe Benefits of Failure, and the Importance of Imagination." *Harvard Gazette,* June 5, 2008. Accessed June 7, 2015. http://news.harvard.edu /gazette/story/2008/06/text-of-j-k-rowling-speech/.

Rudman, Laurie A., and Peter Glick. "Feminized Management and Backlash Towards Agentic Women: The Hidden Costs to Women of a Kinder, Gentler Image of Middle Managers." *Journal of Personality and Social Psychology* 77(5) (1999): 1004–1010.

Rudman, Laurie A., and Peter Glick. "Prescriptive Gender Stereotypes and Backlash Toward Agentic Women." *Journal of Social Issues* 57(4) (2001): 743–762.

Saul, Michael. "Caroline Kennedy No Whiz with Words." *New York Daily News,* December 29, 2008. Accessed June 7, 2015. http://www.nydailynews.com/ news/politics/caroline-kennedy-no-whiz-words-article-1.355586.

Schifferin, Holly H., Miriam Liss, Haley Miles McLean et al. "Helping or Hovering? The Effects of Helicopter Parenting on College Students' Well-Being." *Journal of Child and Family Studies* 23(3) (2014): 548–557.

Schmader, Toni, and Alyssa Croft. "How Stereotypes Stifle Performance Potential." *Social and Personality Psychology Compass* 5(10) (2011): 792–806.

Schneider, Andrea K., Catherine H. Tinsley, Sandra Cheldelin, and Emily T. Amanatullah. "Likeability v. Competence: The Impossible Choice Faced by Female Politicians, Attenuated by Lawyers." *Duke Journal of Gender Law and Policy* 17 (2010): 363–384.

Schweider, David. *The Psychology of Stereotyping*. New York: The Guilford Press, 2004.

Seck, Hope Hodge. "Controversy Surrounds Firing of Marines' Female Recruit Battalion CO." *Marine Times*, July 15, 2015. Accessed September 20, 2015. http://www.marinecorpstimes.com/story/military/2015/07/07/kate-germano-fired-marine-corps-female-recruit-unit-commander/29763371/.

Segrin, Chris, Alesia Woszidlo, Michelle Givertz, and Neil Montgomery. "Parent and Child Traits Associated with Overparenting." *Journal of Social and Clinical Psychology* 32(6) (2013): 569–595.

Seligson, Hannah. "Why the Sting of Layoffs Can Be Harder for Men." *New York Times*, January 31, 2009. Accessed September 13, 2015. http://www.nytimes.com/2009/02/01/jobs/01layoff.html.

Silva, Christine, Nancy M. Carter, and Anna Beninger. "Good Intentions, Imperfect Execution? Women Get Fewer of the 'Hot Jobs' Needed to Advance." Catalyst (2012). Accessed June 24, 2015. http://www.catalyst.org/system/files/Good_Intentions_Imperfect_Execution_Women_Get_Fewer_of_the_Hot_Jobs_Needed_to_Advance.pdf.

Simmons, Rachel. *The Curse of the Good Girl: Raising Authentic Girls with Courage and Confidence*. New York: Penguin, 2010.

Singh, Val, Savita Kumra, and Susan Vinnicombe. "Gender and Impression Management: Playing the Promotion Game." *Journal of Business Ethics* 37(1) (2002): 77–89.

Slaughter, Anne-Marie. "Why Women Still Can't Have It All." *Slate*, July/August 2012. Accessed September 13, 2015. http://www.theatlantic.com/magazine/archive/2012/07/why-women-still-cant-have-it-all/309020/.

Snyder, Mark. "Self-Monitoring of Expressive Behavior." *Journal of Personality and Social Psychology* 30, no. 4 (1974): 526–537.

Sparkes, Matthew. "Christine Lagarde: 'Women Can't Have It All,'" *Business Insider*, September 26, 2012. Accessed September 13, 2015. http://www.businessinsider.com/christine-lagarde-women-cant-have-it-all-2012-9.

Sparks, John R., Charles S. Areni, and K. Chris Cox. "An Investigation of the Effects of Language Style and Communication Modality on Persuasion." *Communication Monographs* 65(2) (1998): 108–125.

Stanberry, Lindsey. "Try This Experiment If You Say 'Sorry' Too Much." Refinery 29, August 3, 2015. Accessed October 3, 2015. http://www.refinery29.com/saying-sorry-at-work#.ozt2o1:J1f7.

Stilwell, Victoria. "Fewer Millennial Moms Show U.S. Birth Rate Drop Lasting." *Bloomberg Business*, September 16, 2014. Accessed September 13, 2015. http://www.bloomberg.com/news/articles/2014-09-16/fewer-millennial-moms-show-u-s-birth-rate-drop-lasting.

Stumpf, Stephen A., and Manuel London. "Management Promotions: Individual and Organizational Factors Influencing the Decision Process." *Academy of Management Review* 6(4) (1981): 539–549.

Sweeney, Brigid. "How Female Execs Can Avoid a NY Times–style Epic Fail." *Crain's Chicago Business*, May 20, 2014. Accessed June 7, 2015. http://www.chicagobusiness.com/article/20140520/NEWS07/140519775/how-female-execs-can-avoid-a-ny-times-style-epic-fail.

Tannen, Deborah. *Talking from 9 to 5: Women and Men at Work*. New York: Reed Business Information, 1995.

Tannen, Deborah. *You Just Don't Understand: Women and Men in Conversation*. New York: Ballantine Books, 1990.

"The Grit Project: True Grit and a Growth Mindset." American Bar Association, Commission on Women in the Profession. Accessed June 7, 2015. http://www.americanbar.org/groups/women/initiatives_awards/grit.html.

"The Kardashians Talk Back to Tweets." YouTube, April 1, 2011. Accessed October 3, 2015. https://www.youtube.com/watch?v=d8jL8qz7dwM.

Thomas, Rachel. "Corporate America Is Not on the Path to Gender Equality." Lean In, September 30, 2015. Accessed October 4, 2015. http://leanin.org/news-inspiration/corporate-america-is-not-on-the-path-to-gender-equality/.

Tracy, Sarah J., and Kendra Dyanne Rivera. "Endorsing Equity and Applauding Stay at Home Moms: How Male Voices on Work–Life Reveal Aversive Sexism and Flickers of Transformation." *Management Communication Quarterly* 24(1) (2010): 3–43.

Trix, Frances, and Carolyn Psenka. "Exploring the Color of Glass: Letters of Recommendation for Female and Male Medical Faculty." *Discourse & Society* 14(2) (2003): 191–220.

U.S. Department of Labor. Women's Bureau, Latest Annual Data, 2013. Accessed June 6, 2015. http://www.dol.gov/wb/stats/recentfacts.htm.

Vedantam, Shankar. "Salary, Gender, and the Social Cost of Haggling." *Washington Post*, July 30, 2007. Accessed September 13, 2015. http://www.washingtonpost.com/wp-dyn/content/article/2007/07/29/AR2007072900827.html.

Warner, Judith. "The Women's Leadership Gap: Women's Leadership by the Numbers." Center for American Progress, August 4, 2015. Accessed September 19, 2015. https://www.americanprogress.org/issues/women/report/2015/08/04/118743/the-womens-leadership-gap/.

Wayne, Sandy J., and Robert C. Liden. "Effects of Impression Management on Performance Ratings: A Longitudinal Study." *Academy of Management Journal* 38(1) (1995): 232–260.

Weeks, Holly. "Taking the Stress out of Stressful Conversations." *Harvard Business Review*, July–August 2001. Accessed June 24, 2015. https://hbr.org/2001/07/taking-the-stress-out-of-stressful-conversations.

Weisberg, Anne. "The Workplace Culture That Flying Nannies Won't Fix." *New York Times*, August 24, 2015. Accessed September 13, 2015. http://www.nytimes.com/2015/08/24/opinion/the-workplace-culture-that-flying-nannies-wont-fix.html.

Whipple, Wayne. *The Story Life of Lincoln: A Biography Composed of Five Hundred True Stories Told by Abraham Lincoln and His Friends*. Whitefish: Kessinger Publishing, LLC, 2010.

Whiteman, Mauro. "PepsiCo CEO Indra Nooyi: 'I Don't Think Women Can Have It All Either.'" *Aspen Idea Blog*, July 1, 2014. Accessed September 13, 2015. http://www.aspeninstitute.org/about/blog/pepsico-ceo-indra-nooyi-i-don-t-think-women-can-have-it-all-either.

Williams, Joan C. "Hacking Tech's Diversity Problem." *Harvard Business Review*, October 2014. Accessed September 13, 2015. https://hbr.org/2014/10/hacking-techs-diversity-problem.

"Women 'Take Care,' Men 'Take Charge': Stereotyping of U.S. Business Leaders Exposed." Catalyst, October 19, 2015. Accessed June 6, 2015. http://www.catalyst.org/knowledge/women-take-care-men-take-charge-stereotyping-us-business-leaders-exposed.

Yip, Jeffrey, and Meena S. Wilson. "Learning from Experience." In *Handbook of Leadership Development*, edited by Ellen Van Velsor, Cynthia D. McCauley, and Marian N. Ruderman, 63–95. San Francisco: John Wiley & Sons, 2010.

Yovetich, Nancy A., T. Alexander Dale, and Mary A. Hudak. "Benefits of Humor in Reduction of Threat-Induced Anxiety." *Psychological Reports* 66, no. 1 (1990): 51–58.

Zaleski, Katharine. "Female Company President: 'I'm Sorry to All the Mothers I Worked With.'" *Fortune*, March 3, 2015. Accessed September 13, 2015. http://fortune.com/2015/03/03/female-company-president-im-sorry-to-all-the-mothers-i-used-to-work-with/.

INDEX

ABOUT THE AUTHORS

Andrea S. Kramer and Alton B. Harris are married, have a daughter in medical school, and are former law partners. Both have served in senior management positions and have in-depth experience with all aspects of personnel management, including recruiting, hiring and firing, individual and team supervision, compensation, and promotion. They have jointly written more than thirty professional and gender-related articles and book chapters, collaborated in mentoring women in a variety of positions and fields, and spoken together to many business and professional groups about gender bias.

Andie is a partner in the international law firm McDermott Will & Emery LLP, where she heads the firm's Financial Products, Trading & Derivatives Group. She is a nationally recognized authority on gender communication, having mentored thousands of women and written many articles on the subject, including coauthoring the American Bar Association's guide, *What You Need to Know About Negotiating Compensation*. Andie cofounded the Women's Leadership and Mentoring Alliance (WLMA) and currently serves as the organization's board chair. She was named one of the 50 Most Influential Women Lawyers in America by the *National Law Journal* and received the prestigious Gender Diversity Lawyer of 2014 award from ChambersUSA. She is chair emerita of the Chicago Foundation for Women.

Al was a founding partner of the Chicago law firm Ungaretti & Harris, now part of Nixon Peabody LLP. At Ungaretti & Harris, Al served at various times as managing partner, executive and compensation committee member, and head of the Corporate and Securities Practice Group. He is an adjunct professor of law at Northwestern University School of Law, and he sits on the board of directors of a billion-dollar technology corporation. Al has served as mentor, coach, and counselor to many successful businesswomen and recently wrote with Andie, "Taking Control: Women, Gender Stereotypes, and Impression Management."

We'd love to hear from you!

Please visit us at AndieandAl.com and sign up for our newsletter, follow us on Twitter @AndieandAl, and join the conversation on Facebook at Andie & Al

 AndieandAl.com

 @AndieandAl

 Andie & Al